Strong Girls, Strong Parents:
A Guide to Raising Teenage
Girls in a New Era

9/24/17
Dear Heather, Mike, + Sarah!
May you continue to be
Strong Women!
Best Wishes
Robin Sulwon

Strong Girls, Strong Parents: A Guide to Raising Teenage Girls in a New Era

Robin Axelrod Sabag, LCSW

ISBN 13: 9781542545907
ISBN-10: 1542545900
Library of Congress Control Number: 2017901479
CreateSpace Independent Publishing Platform
North Charleston, South Carolina

To Dad, for his constant support, guidance, and love during the writing of the book and throughout my whole life.
To Mom, for her example of what a confident woman is. Thank you for guiding me to be who I am today.

Table of Contents

Acknowledgments

So many people have contributed to this work. I am so grateful to my wonderful family and friends for their support throughout this journey. Thank you, Mom, Dad, and my stepfather, Steve, for raising me to be a strong woman and fostering within me a strong sense of self throughout girlhood and into my teenage years. I would not be where I am without your guidance and the self-esteem that you all nurtured in me at such an early age. Dad, I cannot thank you enough for your tireless dedication to helping me see this book through every stage, including its fruition. Your belief in me as a therapist and a writer has inspired me to attain things well beyond my goals. Mom, I thank you for being so supportive and always listening to my stories and ideas. You have an incredible ability to just be present, without judgment. Thank you for capturing what I wrote with your illustrations.

Thank you to my amazing and devoted husband, Micha, for giving me the idea to write a book, when I never believed I could. As always, your optimism motivated me to reach my dreams. Mostly, thank you for putting up with me as I holed away in my office, writing and rewriting—and for watching the kids while I did it.

Thank you to the best children anyone could ask for, Gavriel and Shai, for allowing me space, being patient, and sacrificing activities with me while I wrote this. Thank you for understanding all those times I was writing this book instead of playing with you. You keep asking to read this book, and I hope that one day you will! Your thought-provoking and inspiring questions often sparked my creativity while I wrote.

Much appreciation also to my stepmother, Kathy, who lovingly and skillfully kept my children engaged while I worked on this text.

Finally, and most importantly, none of this would have been possible without my incredible adolescent clients and their families. I feel so honored to have your trust as you allow me to hear your stories. Your strength, openness, and willingness to share your worlds has been my true motivation for writing this book.

Greetings!

Welcome to the wonderful world of adolescent girls! I am Robin, your guide in this journey into adolescence, with its many bumps and hills. I want to start this by saying that I *do* love adolescent girls. I don't think I could work with them or write this book without having a tender passion for this age group and gender. That's not to say that they don't frustrate me at times and push my buttons, but I can honestly say that I *love* this group. As many people can attest, nothing makes me jump at an opportunity more quickly than getting a referral for an adolescent girl to my practice.

As a clinician, I am deeply touched by the good intentions parents have in interacting with their adolescent daughters. Countless times, I have heard, "If only this stage came with a book" or "I was able to get through the baby, toddler, and early-childhood years. Why is this stage so difficult?" Of course, sitting in my chair as an objective third party, it is easy for me to tell parents what they can do differently. I have witnessed the tears and deep emotions shed over the lack of communication and misunderstanding by the two parties, separated by a generational gap.

This book is an attempt to break down the communication and generational gaps and provide the guide these families have sought. I hope to share what I have learned from my clinical practice, the media, and scientific research to communicate with parents who are desperate to help their daughters. So buckle in, get comfortable, and enjoy this journey!

Section 1: Understanding The Developmental Process of Teenage Girls

CHAPTER 1

Understanding the Adolescent Brain

Arielle's mother, Beth, called, pleading for me to see her daughter. Beth informed me that Arielle had been truant from school thirty-two days during the past three months and had been self-mutilating, isolating herself from friends, and refusing to talk to her. When I asked about any recent changes in Arielle's life, Beth stated that she and Arielle's father were in the process of separating. She added that Arielle's father and sister were moving to Germany for her father's job.

Arielle sat in the waiting room of my office with a big pout on her face and paid no attention to her mother. In the midst of texting, Arielle kept her head down and refused to look at me. She was attractive, with wavy brown hair, dressed in skinny-legged jeans and a pair of Uggs. Ignoring my invitation to come into my office, as well as her mother's pleas not to be disrespectful, Arielle eventually let loose with a tirade: "Screw you, Mom! I'll get there when I feel like it. It's your stupid fucking idea for me to come. You're the one who needs therapy, not me."

Beth's face was completely red as she attempted to chastise her daughter while simultaneously apologizing to me.

I decided to step in and said, "Arielle, thank you for coming. I can see you are not happy about being here, but I cannot accept rude language in my office. Why don't you take a few minutes, and when you are ready, have a seat."

Arielle seemed a bit taken aback, and she shuffled forward into my office. Once in my office, she looked embarrassed and apologized for her vulgar behavior.

I was initially casual with Arielle and validated that things seemed pretty rough lately, confirmed that her anger was understandable, and indicated that, perhaps, we could start afresh.

Arielle's initial encounter is not uncommon, and the shifts in emotions are quite frequent during the adolescent years.

Is She Really Nuts?

During the past twenty-five years, there has been an increase in neuroscience research that reveals why the brain functions the way it does. Prior to the studies in neuroscience, the field of psychology theorized that teenagers behaved inappropriately because of poor parenting practices and unpleasant early-childhood experiences, placing most of the onus on the parents (Bradley 2003, 5). This, in turn, led parents to feel guilty and inadequate. Neuroscience has allowed us to see, however, that teens' brains and bodies are actually undergoing massive changes, hormonally and structurally, and that some of their behaviors are not under their control or their parents' control.

Scientists at the National Institute of Mental Health (2011) have concluded that brains do not fully develop until an individual is in her early twenties. The neuroscientists came to this conclusion by doing brain scans of people from childhood to their early twenties.

Why So Gray?

Scientific research revealed that gray matter largely makes up the outer layer or cortex of the brain, which is the part responsible for memory and thought. While early research indicated that the gray volume was higher in the childhood years and fell off as the child matured, more recent research indicates that the gray volume is largest during adolescence (NIMH 2011). This increase in brain matter allows adolescents to develop decision-making skills; however, what we now know is that in the heat of the moment, teenagers can become overwhelmed by their emotions. At this stage, teens rely more on their limbic systems—the emotional part of the brain—rather than on their prefrontal cortex. This can lead to increased frustration and anger, resulting in lashing-out behaviors, such as kicking walls, yelling, and the like.

Scientists found that the area known as the prefrontal cortex, which is located in the front of the brain and responsible for "executive functioning," does the majority of its growing between ages twelve and twenty. This brain region is responsible for making decisions, regulating behavior, mediating conflicts, and making choices. The prefrontal cortex also suppresses urges and orchestrates goals. During adolescence, the prefrontal cortex grows at a speed exceeded only by its development during the early years. Brain scans also indicate that the parts of the brain used to process information develop first, while the parts that process planning and impulsivity are among the last to develop.

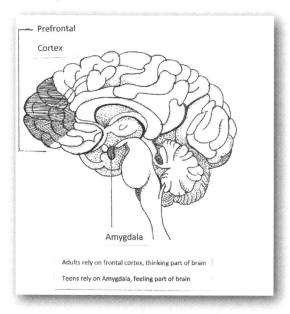

Prefrontal

Cortex

Amygdala

Adults rely on frontal cortex, thinking part of brain

Teens rely on Amygdala, feeling part of brain

Why So Emotional?

In addition to the changes taking place in the brain, there are a multitude of changes taking place in the limbic system, which is the part of the brain that helps regulate heart rate and sugar levels, as well as emotions. The amygdala, an essential part of the limbic system, is primarily responsible for connecting sensory information to emotional responding. Reproductive hormones are also developing during adolescence. These hormones help shape teens' behavior, mood, and brain responses.

Rewards, Rewards, Rewards—Why Teens Need Immediate Gratification

It is also important to note that adolescents value rewards more than adults do. This is due to biological processes taking place in the brain. The reward centers of the adolescent brain are much more active than those of either children or adults.

The combination of the heightened need for stimulation of the reward centers and the role of the prefrontal cortex triggers some of the behaviors we see in teenagers. This might be why teens are so difficult to understand.

For most adults, the notion of jumping from the top of a tower is unfathomable. In adults, the prefrontal cortex kicks in and curbs such impulses, since it is able to take destructive consequences into account. Teenagers, however, may need stimulation of the reward center of the brain. Because the prefrontal cortex is not fully developed, teenagers have more difficulty weighing the consequences of such impulses, and the reward centers may yield to the thrills the teens are seeking. These behaviors occur on smaller scales as well, as is seen when teenagers procrastinate with homework in favor of texting or overspending. Their brains have more difficulty delaying gratification, despite the potential negative consequences.

So What?

You may be reading all this and asking yourself: why is this important? Well, there is good and bad news in all the brain research taking place. The bad news is that rates of impulsivity are higher during the teen years than at any other stage, and decision making and judgment are poorer, since the brain is not yet fully developed. This is also the period in which your daughter is most likely to be exposed to social influences, such as pressure to take dangerous substances. Because there is not yet full maturity in the prefrontal cortex—which, again, is the area responsible for making decisions and judgments—your teenage daughter may be strongly persuaded by outside influences. Unfortunately, the decisions your daughter makes during her teenage years may impact her for the rest of her life.

While it is important for parents to be aware that teenagers may not be as responsible as adults in planning ahead, weighing consequences, and responding to immediate rewards, parents still need to set appropriate limits for their teens. Parents serve their teens best during this stage by being hands-on, and being available to talk and listen, without imposing judgment. Just as when your daughter was a toddler or young child, it is now important—more important than ever—to be consistent with rules, both with your daughter and with yourself. Your daughter is always observing your behavior and is aware of any inconsistencies.

Does this mean that you should not trust your adolescent daughter at all? No. In fact, you should trust her on many levels. This will be discussed later at greater length. However, knowing about her brain is important to understanding where she is developmentally.

The good news is that this is a time when learning can flourish. Because of all of the plasticity and neuron connections taking place in the brain, this is a great time to teach your daughter skills such as reasoning and making good judgments that will be helpful throughout her life. You can also use this time to teach valuable lessons about responsibility. This *cannot* be done by comparing your brain to your adolescent's brain. Adolescents' brains are still developing, and their components, although highly developed in some areas, are less developed in other areas and are not working together in all respects. In adults, various parts of the brain work together to evaluate choices, make decisions, and act accordingly in each situation. The teenage brain doesn't appear to work like this.

Because a teen interprets facial expressions more with her amygdala, the part of the brain responsible for experiencing fear and danger, while adults process emotions with the prefrontal cortex, arguments are more likely to ensue (Bradley 2003, 7). This groundbreaking research on adolescent brain development gives us information as to why it is so essential for parents to encourage their teens to engage in constructive activities. The more exposure your daughter has to activities such as art, music, math, and sports, the stronger the brain connections become during this active period of cerebral growth.

Tips for Building a Healthy Teenage Brain

Although the brain may predispose teenagers to certain behaviors, these responses are *not* hardwired. Behavior is malleable and can change, given the right environment. As a parent, you have a critical role in influencing how your daughter develops. Here are some ways you can help your daughter develop a healthy brain:

- **Encourage critical-thinking skills:** Allow your daughter to think for herself. If she asks you to solve a problem for her, first gently challenge her to try to solve it herself.
- **Foster independence, not dependence:** Help develop a sense of self, or identity, in your daughter. Sense of self entails the ways in which a person views her own traits within the context of the world. Encourage your daughter to take the lead in tasks such as making doctors' appointments

and advocating for herself. Give her tools to be successful, so she is not overly dependent on you.

- **Expect responsible behavior:** It is not unreasonable for your daughter to have responsibilities in the home. Require that she fulfill them before engaging in social activities.
- **Talk through decisions:** Your teen is more impulsive at this age than she will be at any other age in life. Help her slow down and think through decisions, weighing the pros and cons. Do not use shame. Use mistakes as learning opportunities.
- **Be a role model for your daughter:** Although you may not notice it, your daughter is observing what you do and how you do it. If you make a mistake, show her you are human, and use yourself as an example of how you work through problems and evaluate the consequences of actions.
- **Help your daughter find positive outlets:** Whether it's through sports, the arts, writing, or drama, encourage your daughter's expression of the emotions of her unique self.
- **Provide structure:** With all your daughter's afterschool activities, it may be difficult to have dinners together, but try to have family time for at least a half hour a night. It will keep you connected and provide a sense of structure.
- **Have healthy boundaries:** Boundaries make people feel safe and give them a sense of self. Your daughter needs boundaries and limits as a guide to feel safe; this will be a great example of how to negotiate her own relationships. This will be discussed in greater detail in later chapters.
- **Allow your daughter to take some healthy risks in a safe context:** Taking healthy risks will help your daughter mature and become independent. Your daughter needs the tools to assess risks for activities such as camping, rock climbing, and public speaking.
- **Give your teenager some space to breathe:** Although it's important to stay connected, give your daughter some space so that she can experience life. She might resent you or rebel in a destructive way if you are overly protective.
- **Encourage sleep:** Most teenagers are sleep deprived. The more sleep your teenage daughter gets, the more likely she is to make healthy decisions. Encourage your daughter to put away electronic devices an hour before going to sleep.

- **Stay connected with your daughter:** Although it may not always seem so, your daughter more than likely wants to be close to you. Ask her how she is, stay in tune with her needs, and do fun things together. Be available to her.
- **Connect with other parents:** You are not alone in this. Stay in touch with other families, and exchange ideas and resources.
- **Take care of yourself:** Don't let yourself to get burned out. Self-care is always important. Take time for yourself.
- **Find a shared activity that you and your teen daughter can participate in:** Although your daughter may spend less time with you than she did when she was a young kid, do not assume that she no longer needs or wants to spend time with you. Find activities that you both enjoy. These can include going for a walk or a hike, making dinner together, playing a game or a sport, seeing a show, taking a class together, or just having an "us" day.

Tips for Healthy Brain Development (Recap)
ENCOURAGE THESE TRAITS!

- Independence
- Opportunities to weigh risks
- Positive outlets
- Adequate rest
- Responsibility
- Self-expression
- Structure and routine

Having read about the changes taking place in the brain, you may now understand why your daughter may sometimes be quick to act before thinking. Here are some ways you can help you daughter think more carefully:

- Suggest that your daughter take deep breaths if she feels overwhelmed.
- Encourage her to get fresh air.
- Help her relax—encourage her to watch a movie, read a book, or play with the family pet or neighborhood children.
- Encourage your daughter not to talk when she is already fueled with emotion. Wait until she has tried the above methods and is feeling calmer, and then talk through the issues. Trying to work through issues while she is in an emotional state will only make things worse.

Can you think of other ways to help your daughter slow down?

1. _____

_____

_____

_____

2. _____

_____

_____

_____

_____

3. _____

_____

_____

_____

_____

_____

4. _____

_____

_____

_____

_____

5. _____

_____

_____

_____

_____

_____

What are some activities you can engage in with your daughter to encourage critical-thinking skills?

1. _____

_____

_____

_____

_____

2.. _____

_____

_____

_____

_____

3.. _____

_____

_____

_____

_____

_____

_____

CHAPTER 2

Healthy Separation: Leave Me Alone; Wait, Come Back!

I started seeing Monique for individual therapy when her parents were concerned that their once "compliant" daughter was showing signs of distress. She was fifteen years old, the youngest in the family, with two older brothers who were in college. Her grades, which were normally all As, were beginning to slip, and she had recently quit her outside political-activism club without telling her parents. This was an activity she had engaged in since she was a young child. Although she still had a lot of friends and was respectful of her peers and teachers, she was not as accommodating in the home as she once was.

When I questioned the family further, I learned that Monique was arguing with many of the decisions made by her parents, disagreeing with their opinions, coming in past curfew, questioning the rules, and not eating the food that was served, instead making her own meals and eating on her own schedule.

After meeting alone with Monique for several sessions, I learned that she sensed there was a great deal of marital strife between her mother and father and she felt pressure, as the last child in the home, to keep her parents together. Additionally, Monique conveyed that she had no interest in politics and that she was not sure how she felt about her political choices, but that she was only in this club because her parents told her that she was supposed to be "conservative." Monique said that she just got "tired of it all" and was checking out by trying to find her way without succumbing to her parents' rules.

Monique conveyed that her recent behaviors felt even scarier to her and that she feared that by not following her parents' rules, she would lose them altogether, since they would not accept her choices or who she was. This was the only way for her to have her own voice. After intensive family therapy, Monique softened her opinions, which her family did eventually accept.

A Time of Growth and Change

In the instance described above, Monique rebelled in a healthy way and did not resort to other, more damaging behaviors to get her needs met, as may sometimes be the case. Examples of these damaging behaviors include eating disorders, substance abuse, or self-injury. These will be discussed in later chapters.

The process of separation from one's family of origin is a natural stage—one that is necessary for a teenager's healthy development. During this time, individuation also occurs, which is when a person starts to develop a stable personality and a clear sense of who she is, separate from those around her. Although individuation has already occurred in some forms and will continue throughout your daughter's life, the adolescent phase of individuation is particularly crucial. In my experience in working with adolescents and young adults, I have found that when the process of separation and individuation is difficult, the individual may present with challenges in her identity and her interpersonal relationships.

Remember the "terrible twos" when your adoring toddler would run off, only to fly back into your arms for comfort? Well, in case you haven't noticed it yet, that time has come again, only with greater fervor and with absences. The period of separation and individuation is one in which your daughter is renegotiating her relationship with the world and, in particular, with you, her parents.

So now your daughter is not only separating, but she is just beginning to establish her identity. She is not only working toward finding herself, but she is also exploring who she is, separate from her identity within the family. A major question asked during this period is: "Who am I in this world?" It is essential to your daughter's development that she go through this process, since it is healthiest when it is done in the teen years. If it does not happen now, it will happen while she is in her twenties, thirties, forties, or later in life, which can result in developmental problems or relationship difficulties.

How your daughter goes about this process is crucial to her development as an adult, and your role in this process is vital. She cannot do this without pulling away first. The process does *not* have to be a destructive one.

Interdependence Described

Family theorist Murray Bowen (1992, 105) dedicated his work to the study of the differentiation of self as opposed to the idea of fusion. Differentiation is the ability to separate one's feelings and thoughts from other family members'. For example, a highly differentiated self is less likely to be swayed by others' opinions. On the other hand, a less formed person will feel pressured to think or act like others. Such fusion in a relationship or a family can prevent individuation or the ability to develop one's own sense of self. At the other extreme, too much distancing of emotions and connection can result in a remote connection and can lead to cut ties and estrangement in a family.

According to Bowen, individuals who are most fused tend to function poorly and are more likely to be emotionally reactive when stressed. They are at greater risk of not being able to distinguish thoughts from feelings. Additionally, they struggle to differentiate themselves from others, leading to fusion in the family, otherwise known as codependence. Bowen further asserted (1976, as cited in Goldenberg & Goldenberg 1996) that, as individuals marry partners with similar levels of differentiation, they may produce generation after generation of "individuals with progressively poorer differentiation, thus increasingly vulnerable to anxiety and fusion" (Goldenberg & Goldenberg 1996, 178). Poorly functioning parents, according to Bowenian theory, may "seek ways to reduce tension and preserve equilibrium, sometimes at the expense of particularly vulnerable, fusion-prone offspring" (Goldenberg & Goldenberg 1996, 186).

What to Expect

Starting between about ages twelve and fourteen, you may notice that your daughter is pulling away from you. This is essential to her process of becoming a unique individual. Although at times you may not realize it, because it occurs gradually, this has been happening from the minute she was born. After the time of birth, babies become less fused with their mothers, since they no longer need the mother's energy and food to survive.

By the time your daughter is between fifteen and seventeen, you may notice that she is becoming increasingly independent. She may be trying on different identities to see which is the right fit for her. The shift in the relationship with your daughter, combined with her developmental brain changes, hormonal changes, and the influence of new peer groups, can be challenging for you as her parent.

Although this may be hard to witness, since it has its twists and turns, it is essential to her growth. During this time, she is somewhat separate but still connected to you. It is essential to your daughter's growth that she has a sufficient sense of separateness to challenge some of your values and behaviors. Although this phase of development may create stress, it is a natural and expected process toward autonomy. If you can keep this developmental perspective in the forefront of your mind, you will be well equipped to traverse this period with your daughter, being mindful of the challenges and still setting appropriate limits.

Also, note that your daughter's desire to develop a unique identity is not equivalent to her wanting to disconnect from you completely. While your daughter may not be giving you this message, she does, in fact, need you in her life—but in a different way than she did before.

Example of Identity Building

Erica was a bright girl with a burgeoning social life, average grades, and the potential to get a scholarship to play Division I soccer. Her parents were divorced but maintained positive interactions, and Erica split equal time between both homes. She came from a working-class home where both parents had full-time jobs. In her junior year of high school, Erica took a sociology class, where she learned about injustices caused to animals. Shortly after taking the class, she declared that she was a vegetarian. Erica's family knew little about vegetarianism, and most of their meals contained meat. However, they asked her questions about why she made this choice, showed interest in it, and worked with her to help prepare meals that met her needs.

Healthy Separation

The scenario described above is an example of healthy separation. Not all cases of separation and individuation have to entail a major rebellion. Furthermore, rebellion does not necessarily lead to complete separation. Erica made a choice that was different from her family's, yet her parents showed support by asking questions and expressing interest in her choice.

Look at Your Own Process of Differentiation

One way to help your daughter is by looking at yourself and the dynamics of your family of origin. Here are some questions to ask yourself:

- Can I remember when I went through this period that my daughter is now going through?
- What was it like for me when I was separating from my own family of origin?
- Did I feel like I had the space to be my own person?
- Did I feel accepted by my own parents in the choices I made?
- Was I made to feel guilty if I did not call or visit enough as a teen?
- What do I appreciate about how my family handled this period in my life?
- What do I wish my parents had done differently?
- What can I learn from my experience that would help my own daughter?

It is important to keep in mind that you are not your daughter, and she is not you; this is her path. Even if you did wild and crazy stuff when you were her age, it doesn't mean she will follow the same route. Evaluating your own process might help you decide what you would like to do differently for your daughter and what kinds of values you might want to pass on to her.

Evaluating Your Relationship with Your Daughter

It may be harder than ever for you as a parent to let go and change the dynamics of the relationship with your daughter at this time. Although you may want the relationship you had when your daughter was a young child, it is important to think about her needs. Consider the following:

- Do I ever feel threatened by my daughter's developmental changes, because I fear she won't need me as much as she once did?
- Am I putting my daughter's needs before mine in order to avoid something in my own life?
- Is my own intimate relationship suffering, and am I overly connected with my daughter in order to avoid dealing with my own relationship?
- Am I tolerant of my daughter's lifestyle, beliefs, and values?
- Am I okay with my daughter being different from me and making choices that do not fall in line with the rest of the family's pattern?
- Are there unspoken rules within my family that my daughter is expected to follow?
- Do my daughter's appropriate or difficult behaviors define my worth as a person?
- Is my happiness determined solely by my daughter and my other children?

The good news is that answering yes to any of these questions is absolutely normal and okay. Being aware of these feelings as a parent is important. This is a normal process, and your awareness can help you become a more mindful parent in allowing your daughter to separate in a healthy manner.

Negative Consequences of Not Allowing for Separation

- Your daughter may learn that others' needs are more important than her own. She may feel selfish about putting her own needs first.

- She may use you as her role model by looking to others to take care of her feelings, rather than being self-responsible.
- She may feel that she is being controlled by you and act out by withdrawing or exhibiting unhealthy behaviors. As an adult, this may result in her having a difficult time taking responsibility for her own behaviors.

Tips for Helping Your Daughter During This Time

- When your daughter expresses her opinion, show interest and avoid judgmental statements: Say, for example, "That sounds interesting. Can you tell me more about your opinion on this?"
- When she shares information that you may not agree with, say, "Can you tell me more about your point of view?" or "Just because I disagree with you, it does not change my opinion of you. I still respect what you have to say."
- If she makes a mistake, say, "You're navigating life bravely. You're learning a lot, I'm sure."
- When discussing conflict, ask open-ended questions and show empathy: "How is this issue between us causing you to feel?"
- Have a sense of passion and purpose in life outside of your daughter's life. Show your daughter that you can care for yourself, so that she does not feel responsible for you. If you are in a relationship, go out; kids like to see their parents happy. It places a great burden on them when they feel they are the center of your life.
- Define your worth through your own interests; this will place less pressure on your daughter to have to please you. Let her please herself, and you can please yourself.

Can you think of some times when your child's separation was difficult for you? How did you handle it?

_____

_____

_____

_____

_____

_____

Healthy Boundaries

Boundaries, both physical and emotional, are essential to all relationships—whether social, professional, intimate, or familial. The ability to set and maintain these boundaries is necessary to conduct wholesome relationships. Healthy boundaries lead to worthwhile relationships, while unhealthy boundaries can lead to dysfunctional ones. For some, the idea of boundaries may be a foreign concept, while to others it may be more natural. In order to set appropriate boundaries, one must know and understand one's limits.

To start, I will provide a definition of each subset of boundaries:

Physical boundaries entail having a barrier between you and another person. Physical boundaries allow one to protect her own personal space. This may vary according to one's culture. For example, when traveling to different parts of the world, you may encounter others who stand close to you and may not apologize when bumping into you in a crowded area. In other cultures, it is more common to allow a greater distance between people and to be extremely polite if someone enters this personal space. You may remember the _Seinfeld_ episode with the "close talker." In this case, the individual in the sitcom was noted for getting too close for others' comfort level. All joking aside, if one is uncomfortable with the amount of space she has with another person, it is okay to reset the personal distance. More concerning examples of the violation of physical boundaries entail inappropriate touching, unwanted sexual advances, stealing from others, or invading others' privacy by looking through their personal belongings.

Emotional boundaries relate to emotional connections. People with poor boundaries may have difficulty respecting others' emotional space by becoming involved in their affairs when it is not welcome or appropriate. On the job, this could be someone who inappropriately shares personal information with coworkers. It could also be a person in a position of power taking advantage of someone with less power. Blurred boundaries may arise in parent-child relationships. For example, it may be inappropriate for parents to share their personal burdens with their children. Another example is when parents do not allow their children to have their own personal opinions, thus pressuring the children to conform to the parents' positions.

In relationships, comfort levels with boundaries vary with each individual; however, it is important that each person be able to declare her comfort levels and that partners respect each other's wishes in relation to boundaries. Additionally, being a parent does not necessitate giving up individuality in order to bond with your children. A parent may share too much, too soon in many of her relationships. Those with poor boundary control often feel responsible for their daughter's happiness at the cost of their own.

Examples of Unhealthy Boundaries:

- Inappropriately touching someone
- Breaking down emotionally in order to have someone rescue you
- Giving all of yourself at the expense of your own needs
- Taking on tasks that you cannot handle
- Expecting others to know your needs
- Letting others define you
- Feeling responsible for others' feelings, emotions, and happiness
- Being unable to say no, due to fear of rejection or abandonment
- Sharing too much of yourself too soon
- Basing your sense of self on others' perceptions of you
- Not sharing or asking for your needs to be met

Examples of Healthy Boundaries:

- Having a strong sense of self and self-respect
- Communicating needs to others
- Taking responsibility for your needs
- Asserting yourself when treated unfairly
- Protecting physical and emotional space

How to Let Go

Although this period can be difficult for you as a parent, know that in allowing your daughter to separate, you are doing something beneficial for her. As a parent, you can help your daughter by allowing her to learn from her mistakes and find her own way in the world. This process does not require physical distance, just the space to allow your daughter to thrive and become her own unique person.

Section 2: Skills and Character Building

CHAPTER 3
Self-Esteem: Providing Tools to Develop Skills

As the teenage years draw closer, your once exuberant, self-assured daughter may appear more withdrawn or less secure. Before delving into the causes for this, first let's look at the definitions of *self-esteem* and *confidence*.

There are varying views on what self-esteem actually is. The overall sense, though, is that self-esteem entails being okay in your skin. Someone with high self-esteem might say, "This is me, and I am okay with that." Self-esteem describes a person's overall sense of value and self-worth. It reflects her beliefs about herself and the knowledge that she has a place in the world different from everyone else's.

Confidence, however, is the feeling that a person can rely on herself. It is about being able to say, "I'll figure this out." It is about having faith, trust, and self-assurance that "I can succeed." It reflects a person's sense and inherent knowledge that she can accomplish something. Confidence does not develop in a teenage girl by telling her that she is beautiful, intelligent, or likeable. Confidence is built when girls accomplish a task and feel proud of the results. Building confidence entails achieving mastery over something and knowing inside that the person has had many successes in the past and can survive or even excel in a variety of situations in the future. Here is an example that describes how **confidence is *not being fostered***:

Martina, age seventeen, excelled in all areas of school. However, when it came to oral presentations, she described herself as feeling nervous, agitated, and almost "frozen with fear." She had finessed her first four years of school without ever having to orally present. This was made possible because she negotiated with her teachers to complete another assignment in lieu of presenting. Her parents also spoke to her teachers on her behalf and even had the family doctor write a note that Martina's "social anxiety" prevented her from presenting in class. Martina reported that in order to pass one of her honors classes and to continue in her field of study, she would have to speak in public.

Although her parents were well intentioned, helping Martina avoid the presentations did not serve her well or allow her to build mastery over a difficult hurdle. Guiding Martina to face a difficult situation and allowing her to regulate her stress would have enabled her to learn to work through those emotions and face her fears. Martina *did* end up doing the presentation and eventually went into marketing, which required occasional presentations. Girls must be encouraged to persevere in the face of struggle, regulate their emotions, and believe in themselves. They need to make mistakes before solving a problem and learn the skills of relaxing and coping with anxiety.

Low Self-Esteem Described

Low self-esteem can be a cognitive problem in which a person has self-deprecating thoughts and feels that others view her similarly. Once low self-esteem develops, it permeates how a girl views herself and can lead to self-defeating thoughts and, sometimes, even self-destructive behavior. Low self-esteem may start in childhood, but it has the potential to become more extreme during the teenage years.

Naturally, as her parent, you want your daughter to feel good about herself—to be a confident, self-aware young woman with the ability to make good decisions and healthy choices. Girls with high self-esteem make good choices, feel secure in themselves, care about others, and do not try to change who they are in order to make others happy. Research indicates that the behaviors associated with low self-esteem among teenage girls are alarming.

According to the Dove Self-Esteem Fund, approximately 75 percent of girls with low self-esteem have admitted to engaging in activities such as binge eating and purging, cutting, bullying, smoking, or drinking, compared to 25 percent of girls with high self-esteem (PR Newswire 2008). Additionally, statistics indicate that teenage girls with low self-esteem are at great risk for engaging in unhealthy drug and alcohol consumption and unprotected sex (PR Newswire 2008).

What Deflates Self-Esteem?

- **Media portrayal:** Another obvious reason why self-esteem declines during this age is the media portrayal of women. When they view airbrushed images and anorexic-like figures, young women are likely to feel as though they are not up to par with the "ideal" women they see depicted daily.

- **Sexualization of girls:** This can occur through images in the media or through the manner in which peers and the adults in a girl's life treat her. When a girl's worth is derived only from her sexual appeal, her self-esteem and confidence are undermined. This leads to a sense of shame and difficulty in developing a healthy self-image.
- **Relationships:** Teens and parents tend to have more difficulty communicating during this stage of life. Due to a teenage girl's cognitive and hormonal changes, communication becomes more difficult, and a breakdown of the relationship is more common. The weakening of the bond can cause a decline in self-esteem.
- **Fear of appearing conceited:** One message a teenage girl gets is that if she shows confidence, it means she is conceited, which is a characteristic that is particularly under attack by other girls. Girls must understand that feeling good about themselves doesn't meant they are being boastful or conceited.

The following may be signs that your teenager is battling with her low self-esteem:

- **Avoiding social situations:** Peers play a central role during this period of your daughter's life. Teens who have weak bonds with peers may avoid social situations.
- **Overapologizing:** Often, a person apologizes excessively when she does not feel adequate and is essentially saying, "I am sorry for my existence." The girl may be feeling that someone better should be in her place.
- **Averted eyes/drooped body posture:** In Western culture, lack of eye contact is a sign of low self-esteem. This is also true of walking with one's head down. Teenagers who behave in this manner might be avoiding social contact.
- **Engaging in excessive sexual contact:** Teenagers who do not feel good about themselves may seek validation through sexual behaviors.
- **Avoiding physical contact:** Your teenage daughter may not be as cuddly as she once was. However, teenage girls who completely terminate physical affection may have feelings of shame or disgust about themselves and their bodies.
- **Behaving aggressively:** Teenage girls who feel unlovable may act angrily, even aggressively, in order to attain some level of attention.

- **Using negative self-talk:** Teenage girls who talk divisively about themselves, their abilities, or their appearance are communicating that they view themselves negatively.
- **Constantly comparing herself to friends:** It is natural for your daughter to compare herself to her peers. However, if she constantly compares herself to her peers in a negative manner, there is cause for concern.
- **Rejecting compliments:** Many teenage girls sometimes get squeamish when receiving a compliment. However, someone with low self-esteem may deflect or deny *all* compliments.

Low Self-Esteem Presents in Many Ways

Julia appeared to have it all. At fifteen, she was a sophomore in high school. Everyone told her she was beautiful. She skipped a grade, had many opportunities to date, and was on the tennis team. Her parents were married, and she was the youngest of three children. Julia's mother brought her to my office upon the referral of her family-medicine physician, because Julia had been complaining of headaches and a lack of sleep. Medical concerns were ruled out, and it became clear that Julia's concerns were psychological.

After several meetings with Julia and her family, it became evident that Julia had an anxiety disorder. Julia reported feeling constant pressure to perform and exceed standards that she felt were set by her family and friends. Although things appeared perfect on the outside, she did not feel so on the inside. Julia revealed to me that she did not feel capable of doing anything on her own and that her self-worth was based primarily on extrinsic factors such as compliments from others. Even though Julia was constantly told she was beautiful and smart, this did not make her feel any better about herself.

Julia's parents expressed a great deal of confusion as to why Julia felt this way about herself. They stated that they constantly told her how pretty she was and that they were always available to help with her homework. They were so distressed at witnessing Julia's anxiety, they stopped giving her household chores and discussing her grades with her.

I admit, it took some time for me to sort out this somewhat perfect-appearing situation. However, after several sessions of therapy with Julia and her family, it became clear to me that what I was seeing was increasingly common with teens and their families. Julia's constant reminders of her assets did not give her the self-esteem and confidence that would enable her to feel like a capable, competent young woman. What Julia needed was the ability to problem solve on her own, negotiate with teachers without parental intervention, and feel mastery over something. The fact that she was praised for her looks did not allow Julia to feel accomplished or give her the tools to have agency in the world.

Let's look at another example.

Heather was an average student in a home where grades were important, but not the be-all and end-all. Heather was encouraged to try her hardest, but if she came home with less-than-perfect grades, she was not berated. Education was emphasized, and the responsibilities of college and grades were placed on her.

Heather excelled in sports, was an avid camper, and was the captain of the swim team. She was very sociable and participated in school activities and social events. Although Heather was praised for her accomplishments, her feelings of self-worth were not dependent on extrinsic rewards. When Heather had difficulties with friends, her parents did not intervene. They listened, asked questions, and encouraged her to make her own choices. Although she did not have the "perfect" appearance, Heather felt well accomplished and confident.

Her family came to see me because Heather had asked to spend her senior year in Spain with a host family. There were a few instances when Heather was at parties with underage drinking. Her parents wanted to be sure that Heather could keep herself safe while far away from home and make good decisions, particularly given that the drinking age in Spain was younger than in the United States.

I met with the family only a few times, since it was clear that Heather was highly competent and confident and that she had the tools she needed to spend the year in Spain meaningfully and safely. What was most striking about this young woman was that her repeated experiences in problem solving, and the self-awareness she developed through swimming and outdoor activities, gave her the tools she needed to feel confident and self-assured. She was not as accomplished or attractive as many of her peers, but through her engagement in activities, she learned how to lose, be a team player, and work hard to attain mastery over challenges. This led to her feel confident in other areas of her life.

Ways to Help Your Daughter Improve Her Self-Esteem

In order to help your teenage daughter improve her self-esteem, try the following:

- **Look at your own behavior:** Do you find yourself putting yourself down when you are in the presence of your daughter? Do not focus on your appearance or body image. Try not to comment on others' images either, but on their accomplishments and character.
- **Let girls fail:** This requires letting them try, even if they do not succeed sometimes. Protecting girls from experiencing failures, even small ones, can cause girls to feel inept. Allowing girls to experience disappointments builds strength and resilience.
- **Encourage your daughter to soothe herself before you console her and help her to resolve things:** Your daughter needs to be able to build up the emotional tolerance for disappointment without you or someone else doing it for her. If she can learn this skill now, she will be able to use it her entire life. This is how teens learn to self-regulate their emotions. You can't always be there to do for them.
- **Don't try to fix things for your daughter:** As hard as this may be, let your daughter make mistakes. Try not to overprotect or fix things for her. Allowing her to make mistakes is a wonderful way to encourage her to grow and learn from her experiences. (See the previous bullet for reiteration of this point.)
- **Build communication:** If you notice that your daughter seems down, approach her. If she does not feel like talking about what is bothering her, let her know you are always available to talk.
- **Be aware of social media and what messages your daughter is experiencing and assimilating:** Watch shows and media with your daughter. Discuss how girls and women are portrayed. This will be discussed at greater length in future chapters.
- **Encourage math and sciences:** Be aware of games and activities where math and science skills are used. If your town or city offers programs for girls in these areas, get her involved at a young age.
- **Listen to your daughter, and encourage her to speak her mind:** Girls need the skills to speak up and be assertive.

- **Be a role model:** Do not focus on your own body. If you are a woman, do not make remarks about needing to lose weight. Do not comment about other women's bodies. If you are a man, do not talk about your daughter's body, other women's bodies, or your own body. Even small comments can have significant consequences. Women well into their adulthood can often still remember comments made by their parents concerning their figures.
- **Praise your daughter for who she is, not for her appearance:** Instead of emphasizing how your daughter looks, say, "I really liked the way you handled that situation."
- **Be aware of your own gender stereotypes and challenge them:** Ask your daughter to help you fix things in the house, not just make dinner and set the table.
- **Be aware of how you talk about others:** Be sure to send messages that focus on what's inside a person and how we treat others. This is what defines us and makes us who we are.
- **Get dads involved:** Girls with fathers in their lives are likely to have more positive relationships, are more successful and ambitious, are less dependent on others, and are less likely to be in abusive relationships. Dads play a huge role in their daughters' lives.
- **Get your daughter involved in sports and other physical activities:** Getting your daughter involved with sports at an early age can help her appreciate her body for its worth rather than for its beauty. Exercise can also reduce stress and depression and help your daughter feel strong and confident. Regular physical exercise, when it's something they enjoy, can enhance girls' mental health, reduce symptoms of anxiety, and help them feel strong and competent.
- **Pay attention to her activities:** Take an interest in whatever your daughter shows interest in, and help her to develop it.
- **Encourage the outdoors:** Giving your daughter the skills to be outdoors will enable her to have a greater sense of her body and feel comfortable with its strengths. It will also gently push her outside her comfort zone and encourage confidence and a sense of agency. Introduce your daughter to camping, climbing, swimming, and other outdoor activities.

**Describe some ways to help your daughter
improve or bolster her self-esteem:**

CHAPTER 4

Effective Ways to Communicate: Is She Speaking a Different Language?

High-school sophomore Sharon Lee and her parents sat in my office for a family session after a particularly stressful weekend. Sharon's mom reported that Sharon slept at the house of a trusted friend, Amelia, on Saturday night. After Sharon was dropped off, she and Amelia walked to a party being held by a senior boy who lived down the street from Amelia. They returned home at 11:00 p.m., which was later than Sharon's curfew.

Sharon's parents did not know about the party until the following morning, when Sharon related what she had done during the sleepover. Sharon's mother was visibly angry and reported during the session, "It's like we don't even know who you are anymore. This is so unlike you." Sharon responded, "You are just the strictest parents in the world. I can't tell you anything without you freaking out." Sharon's father responded, "We just care about you, and it's our job to keep you safe."

"I don't need you for that anymore. Besides, I did nothing wrong. Amelia's parents said we could go, and her curfew is later than mine," stated an angry Sharon.

Sharon's mother looked at me with an exasperated expression. "It's like everything we say is wrong. Her door is always shut. She's always on that phone, talking or texting. She never wants us around. I don't know what to do anymore. I feel like she's gone."

"Look at me, Mom, not her!" Sharon demanded, sobbing. "You have no idea what you guys are saying. I do need you still. You just don't get it!"

Understanding Your Connection

Connection? Is that even possible? Does raising a teenage girl mean it's time to sit back and accept that you are no longer needed as her parent? What your daughter needs from you as a parent may change in how it looks over the next few years, but you are still very much needed!

Once you have a firm grasp of the concepts expressed in chapters 2 and 3, and you can accept that your daughter is developing into her own person, you will see that she will stay intensely connected to you even as her attention shifts to peer groups, school, and her life's passions. Nothing is more important than the connection you have with your daughter at this stage. The research indicates that the greatest predictor of delay in the onset of teen sexual behavior is the degree of connection the youngster has with her primary caretakers (Advocates for Youth 2010). Additionally, adolescents are at a lower risk for tobacco, drug, and alcohol use and for delinquent behaviors if the connection to their parents is strong (Advocates for Youth 2010). When you are connected, everything comes about more smoothly, and if your daughter acts out (which is inevitable), the connection with her will take less time to reestablish itself.

During adolescence, peers have great influence over teens' behavior; however, parents hold more weight than they sometimes realize. The frustrations that exist among teenagers and parents often abound as a result of communication issues, misunderstanding of behavior, generational differences, and the teen's feelings of being judged or lectured to rather than conversed with. As was described in the scenario above, misunderstandings are common, and often the minute the parents are out of sight, the teens' minds are elsewhere. Do not fall into the trap of believing that your daughter is trading you in for her friends or that rebellion means there is now a disconnect. Although she may be forming a new identity, your daughter does not want to lose her connection with you. Maintaining the relationship will look different and may take more work on your end.

The Evolving Relationship with Your Daughter

Connecting with your daughter as a young child may have seemed a more natural process as you cuddled, played Legos, did art projects, and went on adventures together. The face that once lit up at seeing you may have been replaced by a face with a scathing frown. Although the changes in your relationship were gradual, you may still be left feeling confused. In some ways, your daughter depends on you for everything, and, at other times, she pushes you away and wants nothing more to do with you.

Her main concern during this phase of her life is establishing her identity and fostering her independence, both of which are developmentally appropriate. Therefore, building a relationship with you is not her main focus. Try not to feel slighted if your relationship with your daughter is not as strong as it once was. The fact still remains that your daughter needs you in her life, and communicating that you are there for her is as important as ever. Knowing that the road ahead will be full of ups and downs will help prepare you for what lies ahead. Consider this scenario:

Aisha and her parents were in my office on a Wednesday evening. With her head down and a scowl on her face, Aisha listened as her father described his relationship with his daughter: "It's like she's a split persona. One minute she is holed up in her room, not letting anyone near her. The next minute, she's reprimanding us for not asking us how her day was."

Realizing the irony in this, Aisha slowly lifted her head and burst out laughing.

Understanding Her World

Many factors explain why your daughter's moods may be inconsistent. Aside from the brain and hormonal shifts discussed in chapter 1, a day in your daughter's life is complex. Not only does she go to school, but she has to navigate the pressures that await her in interactions with friends, teachers, and romantic partners. Your daughter lives in a social minefield daily, and she is likely doing her best, given her life, her experiences, and her level of maturity. She is forced to endure all this while appearing attractive and in control. By the time she gets home, she is exhausted and may just need some down time to decompress. The last thing she needs is added pressure and another person to challenge her.

As a parent, however, it may be difficult to read your daughter's cues and new behaviors. Common complaints heard from parents include the following:

- She's always talking to her phone. She never comes out of that girl cave.
- If I try to talk to her about anything, like how her day was, I get a sharp answer and a dirty look. Nothing I say is right.

- She keeps everything inside, but I always hear her whispering to her friends. I am glad she is talking to someone, but when she is sad, I just want to help her. I don't always trust the friends from whom she is seeking advice.
- Every time I do try to give her advice, she snaps at me and storms out of the room.
- She can go from extremely active to almost comatose within minutes.

Teenage girls often make claims about their parents like the ones that follow:

- They always give me the third degree. They ask so many questions about where I am going and who I will be with. It's like they don't trust me.
- It's as if they think I am doing something illegal on my phone. All I am doing is texting my friend to say "Good night." The other day I was using my iPhone to solve a math problem, and my mom almost had my head because she thought I was on Instagram instead of doing my homework!
- Even when I do try to talk to them or ask advice, they give me a whole lecture. This is when I completely zone out.
- Even when I offer an opinion on a subject, my dad has to tell me that I am wrong. It's like he is the expert on every subject, and I have to agree with him. It makes me feel judged when I express an opinion, and then it makes me want to open up even less.

Connecting with Her

While it might be easier to just check out and wait until she is a fully grown, mature adult, connecting with your teenage daughter is essential for her development and a golden opportunity to build on a relationship that will last the rest of your lives. Here are some ways to connect with your daughter:

- **Be loving:** Show care and ways to bond. Make your daughter feel she is just as cherished as when she was a young child. Find every opportunity to connect. Hug her hello every morning, hug her good-bye when she leaves for school, and hug her again when she comes home.
- **Lay off the lectures:** I am sure you have years of wisdom that you can share with her, but your daughter may not be ready to hear about it. Once you start up, her eyes will glaze over, and you will have lost her.

- **Be open to discussing issues such as relationships and sex:** Your daughter is searching for information on these topics, and whether you are her mother, father, or guardian, you are the perfect person to give it to her. Having the conversation will not lead to undesirable behaviors. It will actually deter them. Research shows that children who are connected to their parents feel secure in waiting to have sex. Unfortunately, the teens who do not feel secure look for affection in other places, leading to early sexual relationships. Talking about these topics can help your daughter have a better self-image and can also help her understand how to cope with uncomfortable situations.

- **Focus on constructive actions; ease off on the discipline:** Although they may not always let on to it, teens need praise and positive reinforcement just as much as young children. Keep your interactions with your daughter positive. If she spends a lot time in her room, and the minute she comes out, you ask her, "Why did you get a C on your math test?" she isn't going to want to be out out of her room for very long.

- **Stay present:** Although she may not need the same supervision as before, being home with your daughter when she is home can be comforting. She might need to talk; being there can be helpful.

- **Try not to overreact:** If your daughter is open with you and shares something sensitive, keep your anxiety in check. Refrain from yelling or having other intense reactions that can cause her to shut down and not want to share with you again. Try to ask open-ended questions that allow her to process her behavior. For example, you can ask, "How do you feel about what happened?" or "How do you feel the situation may have been handled differently?" If your daughter tells you that she tried a cigarette, you may disapprove, but try not to overreact. If you do, she is less likely to share information with you in the future.

- **Hang around your daughter during times she is more alert:** Teenagers have different biological clocks than the rest of us. If your daughter is watching late-night TV or hanging out in the kitchen past 11:00 p.m. on the weekend, join her, and let a conversation develop naturally. You may be surprised by how easily the conversation may flow.

- **Create opportunities to converse:** I would advise against scheduled conversations, since most teens resist communicating in a forced manner. Teens have different times they like to talk, whether it is after school, before bed, or in the car. Try to be in tune with your daughter's time, and don't be disappointed if it doesn't happen when you want it to happen.

- **Be appropriate with social media and texting:** Don't post things to embarrass your daughter. Also, don't harass and send an excessive number of texts to your daughter. Keep the communication simple. Let her know you are available, but don't overuse texting as a way to try to communicate.

- **Don't compare her to others:** I know how easy it can be to compare your daughter to her friends, parents, family, and especially siblings, but don't do it. Remember, this is the time that youngsters are establishing their identity, so any comparison may make your daughter feel as if she is falling short.

- **Let your daughter have friends over, or allow a friend to come on a family trip:** Since peers are so important during this time, inviting a friend along will allow your daughter to remain connected to her peers, while still enjoying family time.

- **Ask your daughter to teach you something:** Having her show you something will demonstrate that you are taking an interest in her life. Let her teach you about something she is learning in school or ask her to help you with technology.

- **Stay silent at times:** If you notice small mistakes or imperfections in your daughter, try your best to keep this information to yourself. Your daughter may already be hard on herself, and because teens are concrete thinkers, minor criticisms might be confused with general disapproval.

- **Listen:** When she does open up to you, listen with love! Don't give advice all the time. Sometimes, just be there and listen. This is a perfect opportunity to connect and hear what is on your daughter's mind. She doesn't need you to step in and solve all her problems for her. Sometimes she just needs you to be a sounding board. Try to ask a few questions, but don't give her all the answers.

- **Ask smart questions:** To go along with the point above, try to ask your daughter more specific questions. For example, ask her what people thought of her science project, or who is running for student council, rather than asking broad questions such as how her life is going.

- **Keep on trucking:** Don't give up on your daughter. Ever. Even when if it seems like an uphill battle, keep on showing interest in her life.

Listening

Teenagers often complain that when they *do* try to talk to their parents, their parents don't listen without judging or giving their opinions. A key point in getting your daughter to talk is showing her that you are able to listen and validate her feelings. Here is an example of a situation where a parent had difficulty doing so:

Fourteen-year-old Abby started treatment when she and her father lost Abby's mother to cancer several years earlier. On occasion, Abby's father accompanied her to sessions to check in. One day, her father stated, "Abby, you seem kind of distant lately. You didn't even look up when I picked you up from school today."

After some prompting, Abby said, "I've been pretty bummed. Trish and Sareeta have been total bitches lately. They never include me in anything. It's like ever since we started high school, I'm not cool enough for them anymore."

Abby's father laughed and said, "Phew, that's a relief. I never liked them anyway. They are bad news."

Abby looked even further agitated and said, "Well, I did."

Her father said, "Time to move on, sweetie. You have nicer friends like Brooke and Sage. I think this is actually a good thing."

Abby was visibly frustrated and shouted to me, "This is why I don't like to talk to him!"

Her father appeared fully perplexed.

In the above scenario, Abby's father was well meaning, and his intention was to make his daughter feel better. He wanted to ease Abby's pain and lighten her mood. However, by dismissing her distress, he unknowingly added to it. After a few weeks of work, the conversations went more like this:

Abby's father: Abby, you seem kind of down lately.

Abby: Yeah, my friends Trish and Sareeta have been excluding me.

Abby's father: Oh, I can see how that must make you feel awful. You've been friends with them for so long.

Abby: Yeah, it does, and it's like they don't even talk to me now that we're in high school.

Abby's father: (Puts his arm on her shoulder) I know, sweetie. You guys go way back.

Abby: Yeah, but maybe they aren't such great friends if they are going to be that way. I'm lucky to still have Brooke and Sage. They've been by my side during everything we've been through with Mom.

In the above instance, Abby's father didn't tell her how she should feel about the situation. He simply validated her reactions and helped her put words into feelings. For example, his stating "that must make you feel awful" validated her frustration with the situation with her friends. Thus, Abby was able to come to her own conclusion about the situation with her friends. If her father had defined her friendships, Abby may have been less likely to accept this reality.

Challenges; Staying Connected while Setting Limits

It is likely your teenage daughter will face challenges in which she will need you to step in and set limits. Do not let your fear of losing a connection with her stop you from setting limits with her. Limits provide security. Children whose parents do not set limits can feel unsafe and not cared for. Your daughter wholeheartedly needs you to set these limits. When done in a loving, supportive way, setting limits can maintain and even strengthen your connection to your daughter.

When setting limits with your daughter, be mindful that name-calling and giving orders will only serve to push your daughter farther away. Yes, it is important that she learn to accept responsibility for her actions; however, imparting this lesson in the proper manner is essential.

Consider Other Options Than Punishment

If not done carefully, punishment can have long-lasting negative consequences on children of all ages. This is not to say that limits and consequences should not be carried out. However, instead of instilling responsibility in your child, overly harsh punishments only create resentment (Banks 2017). Most forms of punishment—such as hitting, grounding, and yelling—serve to exacerbate behaviors in ways that would make children become more creative about not getting caught. Additionally, excessive punishment can harm a child's sense of self-worth and potentially lead to antisocial behavior, poor school performance, and delinquent behaviors.

What are some ways you were disciplined as a teenager?

_____

_____

_____

_____

_____

What effect did these parental interventions have on you?

_____

_____

_____

_____

_____

Alternative Tips to Help Set Fair Limits With Your Daughter

- **Resolve the conflict quickly:** When having a conflict with your daughter, don't let things simmer or wait for her to apologize; go to her first. Making the first move is a major concession in all relationships. By doing so, you are teaching your daughter a lifelong lesson about how to navigate relationships and resolve conflicts. Your daughter needs to see you as being able to resolve conflict, a skill that is important for her to learn in her own relationships. Be sure to repair the damage quickly and not let tensions fester.

- **Be clear about what the rules are:** Communicate the rules with your daughter when you are both in a calm place, not when either of you is upset. Let your daughter have a say in some of the rules as well. Put the mutually agreed-upon rules in writing so she can see them and so that there will be no inconsistencies in interpretation.
- **Be clear with requests:** Don't make vague requests. If you would like your daughter to straighten her room, explain what that means. For example, say, "Put your clothes in the laundry" or "File the papers on your desk" or "Put your glasses back in the kitchen."
- **Be consistent and fair:** Don't add rules at the last minute just because you feel like it. Stick to the rules that you previously laid out, and deliver fair consequences if they are violated. The rules should be so clear that the consequences shouldn't come as a surprise if the rules are violated.
- **Give independence in increments:** Let your daughter work up to getting more privileges as she proves her maturity. The more responsibly your daughter behaves, the more leeway you can give her. Start with offering a choice, such as which jeans to buy within a price range, and then let her choose other clothing when she proves that she can shop appropriately. Choices allow teenagers to feel that you trust them and that they are part of the decision-making process. Another incremental privilege you can communicate to your daughter is that although she cannot go alone to a party with friends, she is welcome to invite friends over the house.
- **Communicate and follow through on the consequences to your daughter's actions:** If you tell your daughter to be home by 11:00 p.m., and she comes home well after that time, follow through with a consequence. If you do not keep to your word, you will lose some credibility. Be sure that the consequence is reasonable and fits the violation. For example, don't take her phone away for ten weeks, which would be extreme and has nothing to do with breaking curfew. A more reasonable consequence might be to require her to stay home for the next two weekends.
- **Express your feelings:** If you are worried about your daughter's safety, instead of placing blame on her character, make an "I" statement. State something like, "I worry about you when you say you are going somewhere

and don't call when you get there. I know you might feel safe, but you are a new driver, and I need to know if you arrived safely."

- **Emphasize that you will put her safety and health above all else:** It is your job to keep your daughter healthy and safe. Adolescents have a tendency to believe that they are invincible and that no harm can come their way. Thus, they often engage in risky behaviors and do not consider the consequences. Let your daughter know that you will do everything in your power to keep her safe and that if you find that she is engaging in risky behavior, you will have to set much firmer limits.

- **Try not to personalize:** Teenage girls can be experts at going for the jugular. Your daughter may give you constant reminders about how out of touch you are. Don't take it personally. Just stay mindful, and take deep breaths while she continues to push and pull you. It may be helpful to compare this to the tantrum phase of two-year-olds. If you personalize her comments, you run the risk of pushing your daughter away at a time that she needs connection with you the most.

- **Focus on the present:** When in conflict, don't bring up past incidents. Stay in the moment. Teenagers see each occurrence as an isolated event.

- **Remember, you are the parent:** It may seem unfair that you are doing the majority of the work in the relationship with your daughter, but that's what parenting often is. Although she sometimes may look and act like an adult, you have to remember that your daughter is still a youngster. The lessons she will learn when you stay in the parent role and avoid getting too triggered will be invaluable, and your support for her in this journey will strengthen the relationship in the years ahead.

- **Offer choices:** Wherever possible, give choices. If your daughter is having difficulty completing homework on weekends, demanding that she finish all her work on Saturdays may make her feel cornered. Give her the choice to decide during which period of the weekend she will complete her work.

- **Give the conversation back to her:** If you have addressed a difficult topic, such as the discovery that your daughter tried alcohol, make your comment on the topic, express your concern, and then invite her to offer her opinion. State something like, "I'd like to know your thoughts on this behavior."

Just remember, your daughter relies on your attunement, presence, and confidence in her more than she will ever let on. Once you can figure out the best ways to connect with her, you will develop the rhythm that works best for your family. Although there will be some bumps in the road, it is worth the trial period. When you find the best ways to connect with your daughter, your bond will grow and deepen.

CHAPTER 5

Assertiveness: How to Help Your Daughter Speak Her Mind

Teenagers often appear carefree and uninhibited. They may not think twice about sending out nude selfies or having casual hookups. However, when it comes to asserting themselves, many teenagers, particularly girls, struggle in this area.

Example of Passive Behavior

Ashley, age fifteen, was a "nice" girl. I had been seeing her for about five months, ever since she had asked her parents to see a therapist, saying she wanted someone to talk to. Her parents were not entirely sure why she wanted to talk to someone, since there were no major presenting problems, but they allowed her to seek treatment anyway. I was initially uncertain, as well, as to her intentions in coming to therapy.

However, as time unfolded, it became increasingly clear that Ashley had difficulty with self-esteem, had experienced some depression, and had been faced with some unwanted attention from boys in her school. Whenever she came to see me, she was extremely polite, slightly awkward, and overly accommodating. I had to be mindful of not changing my appointments with her in order to schedule other clients, since she would never protest if I did. Throughout my time with Ashley, it became obvious that she was apologetic for her very existence. She had trouble speaking up when her rights were violated; people took advantage of her; and she seldom took her own needs into account. By contrast, Ashley's mother was very assertive, consumed a lot of psychological space, and often wanted to be in the room during the sessions. Her father was a bit more passive, and she and her father seemed to be more connected.

What Does It Mean to Be Assertive?

Assertiveness is a way to express your needs. It is a method to communicate desires, needs, and boundaries. Often when I talk to girls about being assertive, they indicate a fear that they will be viewed as being rude or aggressive. Therefore, I make it clear that although someone may not always like it when you assert your opinion or needs, assertiveness is not about being rude or intentionally hurting someone. It is about making your needs clearly known and asking others to respect them. In order to delineate this for girls, I show them this chart:

	Passive	Aggressive	Assertive
Definition:	Has difficulty asserting honest feelings and thoughts. May express them in an indirect way such as agreeing to do something she does not want to do.	Expresses feelings and opinions in a punishing, threatening, or hostile manner.	Communicates feelings and thoughts in an open manner without violating the rights of others.
Characteristics:	Often sends mixed messages, resulting in misunderstood communications. Tends to allow others to infringe on her rights.	May use humiliation tactics or criticize or blame others. Infringes on the rights of others and takes little responsibility for her actions.	Is able to stand up for her rights without violating others. Is confident, respectful, and nonapologetic.
	Exhibits poor eye contact and tense, slumped body posture.	Has piercing eye contact and an overbearing posture.	Looks at others in the eye when speaking. Speaks clearly and firmly. Stands with erect, grounded posture.
	May speak softly or apologetically.	Speaks in a loud, demanding, and threatening voice.	Speaks clearly and in a loud enough voice for others to hear.

	Passive	Aggressive	Assertive
	Often agrees with others despite her real feelings.	Considers her feelings to be the only important ones and makes decisions without consulting others.	Is collaborative and keeps to the point.
	In a conflict, does not speak up for herself, or does so in a passive, unclear way	Uses "you" statements, which do not put responsibility on herself, but on others. For example, "You always interrupt me."	Uses "I" statements, which take ownership for how she feels, rather than placing responsibility on others. For example, "I feel frustrated when I am interrupted."
Examples:			
	"If I say how I feel, people won't like me."	"I get what I want when I want it, and I don't care who I have to hurt along the way."	"I have the right to say how I feel, but I will do so in a straightforward, respectful way."
	"People never consider my feelings."	"I'm entitled, and you owe me."	"I often feel heard and respected in relationships, and when I don't, I make the conscious choice not to stay in a relationship that does not allow for that."
	"I don't really care what we do, so I leave it up to others to decide. It's easier that way, but then I get resentful."	"It's my way or the highway. I have the final say."	"I have an opinion as to what I want to do and will share it, but I will also consider the concerns of others."

Viewing this table can help teen girls see things more clearly. People often view being assertive as being aggressive, a personality characteristic that most teenage girls do not want. In sum, being assertive means someone is able to

- ask for what she wants or needs,
- disagree in a respectful way,
- give an opinion or say how she feels,
- offer her ideas and recommendations,
- say no without guilt, and
- speak up on someone else's behalf.

It is not the norm in many cultures for girls and women to be assertive. Girls have been socialized to believe that in order to fit in, they must conform to being the standard "nice girl." The problem with teaching girls to be "nice" is that we are not teaching them to stand up for themselves, to make their needs known, and to voice their opinions—all of which are skills they will need throughout the teen years and in adulthood.

Why Is Assertiveness Important?

An assertive communication style can help girls get their needs met. Beyond that, assertiveness training shows girls that they respect themselves and will send the message that others must do the same. Teenage girls who are assertive communicate that they believe in themselves. They're not timid; they are not pushy; and they are confident that their feelings and ideas matter.

Messages from teachers, friends, and the media often depict the way girls are "supposed" to interact with others. As her parent or caregiver, you can teach your teen differently. Girls are socialized to focus on relationships. Research indicates that as early as the preteen years, girls participate less in class and are less likely to state an opinion than boys are. At this age, they are already on the way to putting others' needs first.

Accommodating/passive girls may

- put their own needs last;
- have difficulty resisting drugs and alcohol;
- not raise their hands or participate in class to give answers, voice their opinions, or ask questions;

- struggle to set limits in sexual encounters;
- put up with inappropriate behavior; and
- have a hard time communicating with others.

Assertive girls usually

- make their needs clear;
- participate in class, a behavior that is highly favorable in most school settings;
- can set limits and say no to drugs, alcohol, and sex;
- do not put up with inappropriate behavior and will confront those who treat them disrespectfully; and
- communicate clear and direct messages without apologizing.

Look at Your Own Development

Whether you are the mother, father, or caregiver, consider your own thoughts about girls, your own assertiveness style, and how you interact with others.

What messages did you receive as a child about how girls should behave?

_____

_____

_____

_____

_____

_____

_____

_____

_____

_____

What lessons did you learn about asserting yourself, challenging others, and expressing your needs?

_____

_____

_____

_____

_____

_____

_____

_____

An important component of assertiveness training is teaching your daughter how to say no when it is appropriate to do so. Talk to your daughter about trusting her instincts in various situations, and give her the tools to say no, even if she leaves others feeling dissatisfied. For example, if your daughter tells you that she changed seats on the train because someone sat too close to her, causing her to feel uncomfortable, praise her. Tell her, "Way to follow your gut feelings. I am glad you put your welfare first without worrying about hurting someone else's feelings!" Use these opportunities as a chance to talk to your daughter about advocating for her right to feel safe and put her needs first. Teens, in general, do not like to make a big deal about fears and tend to minimize safety concerns.

This discussion can be followed by role-playing different ways to get out of uncomfortable situations—yell for help, make a phone call, or ask someone to walk her to her car. This can be complemented by going with your daughter to a safety or self-defense class. The main point is to support your daughter in trusting her instincts and asking for help at an age when this can be challenging. The following is an example of an effective role-play that a father used with his daughter who was upset about her situation on the soccer team.

****** *Before the Role-Play*******

Father: Are you okay, Josie? You seem kind of down today. Want to talk?

Josie: Not really, I'm just pissed about soccer.

Father: Want to tell me about it?

Josie: My soccer coach keeps putting me the in the goal. I just want to be a fullback again, but Trina and Carrie are playing there. I practiced that position the whole preseason. I am the first one at practice and the last to leave. I work the hardest, and I don't get to play where I want to. Worst of all, the coach doesn't even pay any attention to me. If I make a suggestion or ask to play fullback, she just ignores me and acts like I'm not even there. I don't even want to play anymore. I'm thinking of quitting soccer.

Father: (supporting and validating) That sounds like a really difficult situation. Have you considered talking to your coach about it?

Josie: What would I even say? It's not like she would care. Plus, I don't like asking for things. It feels too pushy. Taryn is always telling people to give her things, and she is known as the school bully.

Father: I'm not sure if your coach would or wouldn't care. But you won't know unless you ask. Besides, you can ask for what you want without being aggressive. Want to give it a go?

Josie: I guess. We had a cheesy workshop in health class about assertiveness, and they talked about "I" statements, and something stupid like that. I guess I could try.

Father: Great, let's go.

****** *Role-Play*******

Josie: Coach, thanks for agreeing to meet with me after practice. I really like being on the team, but it's hard for me not to play fullback anymore. It's what I'm used to and what I've played my whole life. I miss it.

Father: (as the coach) Listen, Josie. We need you to think about the team, and this is where we need you. If you don't want to play anymore, that's your choice, but we need you in goal.

Josie: (deep breath) No, Coach. I *do* want to play. I love playing soccer and being on the team. I just thought maybe it would be possible to, um, maybe sub or something, if you can, I don't know, for a little, so I can play both, if that works for you? (looking down)

Father: Hmm, I don't know. You are our only player who can play in the goal. You know, anyone can be a fullback, but you have the real skills to be a goalie. I think you need to take this one for the team.

Josie: Um, okay. Thanks.

Father: Great, see you at the game. (walking away)

Josie: Wait, Coach. (head up, making eye contact) I get that you think I have potential. However, I feel frustrated about not being able to play full-back. I would really appreciate it if you would consider subbing me in for Trina for at least fifteen minutes per game so that I have the chance to play fullback as well as goalie. This will give me a chance to see the whole field for when I am in goal. Please consider that. Thank you for listening.

Father: Okay, Josie. That's not a bad solution. I hadn't thought of it that way. I'll put some thought into it.

Additional Tips for Helping Your Daughter Be Assertive

- **Teach her to use "I" statements:** As shown in the example above, "I" statements are an excellent use of assertive communication. Using "I" statements, rather than "you" statements, allows the speaker to place the onus for her feelings on herself. For example, the speaker would assert her feelings by saying, "I feel really scared when…" rather than "You scare me."

- **Model assertive behavior:** Let your daughter see you assert yourself. Show her that it is okay to say no by saying no yourself. Let her see you in situations where you express your needs appropriately.
- **Encourage your daughter to speak for herself:** If your daughter is upset about an interaction or needs to deal with a difficult situation and asks you to do it for her, don't jump in to rescue her. Tell your daughter she is very capable of handling things. Give her encouragement and skills, and, if necessary, practice what she can say or do.
- **Give your daughter opportunities to practice at home:** Encourage her to use her voice at home and practice on family members. Tell her she can express her opinion in a respectful way if there is something with which she disagrees. As her parent, be aware that she may not come across well initially and might even sound aggressive, but be patient if this is new for her, and praise your daughter for expressing her opinions.
- **Role-play:** Give your daughter practice expressing her needs and asking for what she wants. If she is able to practice, she can troubleshoot what may occur and learn ways to handle the situation. This can also help her develop confidence in situations where being assertive is necessary.
- **Actively listen to and validate your daughter when she shares instances of not being heard:** If your daughter shares with you the concern that others do not respect her feelings or rights, take the time to listen to her. The last thing you want to do is exacerbate this feeling by not actively listening to what she has to say. For example, if your daughter tells you that she tried to stand up for herself with classmates who were teasing her, actively listen and respond with empathy. Don't say, "Well, they are not good kids anyway. I don't know why you even care about them." Instead, listen attentively and then validate that it must have been a difficult experience but that you are proud of her for standing up for herself.
- **Help your daughter to believe she has a right to be assertive:** Have your daughter draft an Assertiveness Bill of Rights that lists her personal rights, and post it on the wall as a visual cue. Such a document might include statements like the following:
  - I have the right to say no.
  - I have the right to express all my feelings, whether they are positive or negative.
  - I have the right to not get involved in my parents' disputes.

- ○ I have the right to be in a nonabusive relationship.
- ○ I have the right to my own feelings.
- ○ I have a right to put my needs first.
- **Know when to back off:** If asserting her needs is a real struggle for your daughter and it is taking her some time to learn these skills, give her time. Let her talk about and process her feelings, and don't excessively focus on her achieving these skills. In the example above, it's okay for Josie's father to intervene if she first tries to speak to the coach and gets nowhere, but Josie should observe and learn from the interaction, which would then become a teachable moment.
- **Teach your daughter about assertive body language:** Teach your daughter that she can display assertiveness not only with words but also through the way she presents herself. Teach her to stand tall and look others in the eye and to remain firm, with a serious facial expression, when making a request of someone.

The more your daughter becomes versed in assertiveness skills, the more her confidence will grow and the less she will excessively accommodate the needs of others. With your help, and with other positive role models, your daughter can become empowered to feel in control of her life, make positive choices, and feel good about herself.

Section 3: Common Concerns and Tools to Deal with Them

CHAPTER 6
How to Help Girls Appreciate Their Bodies

Body image. This is a difficult topic for teens, parents, and—believe it or not—therapists to grapple with. Having worked at a residential treatment facility with girls and women with eating disorders, I found one of the toughest issues to contend with was when a client was struggling with her body image. One would think that specialists in the field would have a handful of tools to help someone to cope with and recover from this problem, but when faced with a girl in the midst of body-image struggles, the most common response was to refer the patient to an art or music therapist to "try a different modality." The truth of the matter is that the majority of Americans, particularly women, have struggled with body-image issues at one point or another in their lives. When it comes to helping girls address this problem, many of us are left feeling helpless and confused.

We hear more and more that people are dissatisfied with their body images. *Glamour* magazine's 2014 study found that 54 percent of women were unhappy with their bodies, while 80 percent said that they felt bad when looking at themselves in the mirror. Teenage girls are prime examples of this problem. One study showed that 62 percent of adolescent girls reported wanting to be thinner (Moy 2015, 18). Other studies show that children as young as eleven—and, sometimes, even younger—have body-image difficulties. More alarming is that fact that several studies have indicated that some six-year-olds have wanted to emulate their older peers in their desire to be thinner (Moy 2015, 18.).

Starting as early as five years old, girls can develop negative feelings and attitudes about their bodies (Knafo 2016, 2). During the preteen years, girls often become increasingly aware of their physical appearance and may regard it as a measure of self-worth. Body-image concerns tend to peak at adolescence due to the physical changes that come with puberty. Girls become especially self-conscious about their weight at this time, since their growth spurts have ended and hormonal shifts may cause their bodies to store more fat, particularly in the hips, thighs, and buttocks. This can further cause girls to develop feelings of shame and poor body esteem. Girls who mature earlier may experience body-image dissatisfaction sooner, and the problem may be long lasting (Raising Children Network 2017).

What Is Body Image?

Body image, or body esteem, often reflects how someone feels about her body and about how attractive she perceives herself. When we hear the words "body image," what often comes to mind is how a person feels in relation to her attractiveness, shape, beauty, and weight. However, body image means much more. I often ask my clients, particularly those who are currently struggling with eating disorders or who are in recovery, what they mean when they say are experiencing problems. What I have learned from their responses was initially a bit of a surprise.

Body Image Concerns

Ariana was referred to me by her dietician for preventative work. She had recently lost fifteen pounds following a jaw surgery that restricted her to a temporary liquid diet. The surgery occurred during the summer. When she returned to school in the fall, Ariana was greeted with a great deal of praise for the weight loss. Ariana expressed a desire to continue the liquid diet after the prescribed time, at which point her parents became concerned that their daughter's desire to lose more weight might lead to more extreme weight loss. Subsequently, Ariana lost an additional ten pounds, which was the point at which the dietician and I began working with her.

Ariana came to my office after being on a new meal plan prescribed by her dietician one month earlier. At this point, Ariana had regained seven of the twenty-five pounds she had lost. Because she weighed more than her ideal body weight prior to the surgery, Ariana's weight loss was not anywhere near the cutoff point that would indicate anorexia. However, if she continued losing weight, she could very well have been at risk.

Ariana looked in silence for what seemed like an endless amount of time. After a great deal of prompting, she finally stated, "I just feel awful. My body image is horrible. I feel huge. It's like I can't look at myself now. I just felt so good being smaller for that short time, like I finally fit in. I no longer had to crop my Instagram photos, I got so many "likes," it was like I was starting to finally be somebody, and now it's gone again."

As is clear in the case of Arianna, body image or body esteem is more than how someone perceives her own appearance. We cannot talk about self-esteem without mentioning body esteem, which represents one's mental and physical persona and feeling of self-worth. It embodies how a person feels in her body and the way in which she moves in the world. Body image is based more on feeling than on fact. It is established by self-observation and by being aware of how others react to one's body.

However, in order for a girl to love her body, she must learn to treat it with respect. The way an individual feels about her body can influence the choices she makes in life, the impressions she creates, whom she dates, etc. Having a good relationship with her body allows a girl to view her internal capabilities, rather than external ones, as a reflection of her worth. If a teen wants to feel better about her body, she may not be able to change how she appears, but she can improve the relationship she has with herself.

Risk Factors for Negative Body Image

Although anyone can be susceptible to developing body-image issues, the following are some risk factors for developing more serious problems:

- A family history of disordered eating
- Perfectionist behaviors
- A history of being teased or bullied by peers for appearance
- Pressure from family and peers to conform to an ideal image that equates thinness with beauty
- Excessive social networking
- An already low self-esteem
- Inclination toward depression
- Belonging to a sport or dance group that emphasizes a certain body type
- Having a physical disability

The way in which a girl views her body can be influenced by a variety of factors, including family, skin tone, ability or disability, attitudes of peers, the media, and the fashion industry. Cultural background also factors into views about ideal body shapes and sizes. When considering your daughter's experience with her body image, think about what influenced you as child.

When you were a teenager, what were your thoughts on how your body was supposed to look?

_____

_____

_____

_____

_____

_____

Whatever the case, it is important to be in tune with what your daughter is feeling in relation to her body. The following are tips for assessing whether your daughter is having body-image concerns:

- **Listen:** Listen to how your daughter talks about her body. Notice whether she is excessively self-critical or talks constantly about wanting to lose weight. Be aware of whether she is making comparisons to others or speaking about her body parts in negative ways (e.g., "My thighs are huge and gross. I can't wait to lose fifteen pounds, so I don't look like such a whale."). Teenage girls may speak more subtly (e.g., "My stomach looks bloated today."), refer to a disliked body part, or obsess about weight loss and exercise. Make use of these comments when considering a starting place for further exploring your daughter's perceptions of her body image.
- **Ask questions:** Gently ask your daughter her thoughts on her changing body image in a nonconfrontational way.

Depending on what you learn from her responses, the following tips might be useful in addressing these issues:

- **Acknowledge the feelings your daughter is having about the changes in her body:** Not all girls respond in the same manner to puberty. Some feel a sense of loss and grief. Your daughter may need to work through these feelings. She may show signs of sadness, irritability, and depression. It is important to acknowledge these feelings and reach out in a supportive way by continuing to connect with your daughter and by being affectionate. Just because her body is changing, it does not mean she does not want you in her life. If you pull away from her, her sadness and shame may increase. Remain a constant source of love and acceptance.

- **Be a positive role model:** This includes being aware of how you view your own body. You may have learned your attitude about your body from your own parents. Consider the legacy you want to pass on to your daughter. If you constantly verbalize criticisms about your own body, your daughter is certain to be aware of these attitudes. Instead of putting yourself down, let your daughter hear self-praise. Focus the praise not on the appearance of your body, but on its usefulness. For example, "I love my legs, because they are strong and get me places fast" or (for mothers) "I love my belly, because you lived there." If you weigh yourself obsessively, your daughter is likely to observe, internalize, and perform the same behavior. You don't have to give up the bathroom scale, but consider weighing yourself weekly, and when you do, do not grunt or groan when you notice your weight. If you have not been a good role model in this area, it is not too late to change.

- **Be in tune with your own tendency to compare your body to others' and to your daughter's:** It's hard to compare yourself with other people when you see images of *Sports Illustrated* models (if you are a woman) or various male athletes (if you are a man) and not feel inadequate. If this is an issue, acknowledge this feeling to yourself—but not to your daughter. If you find yourself comparing your body to your daughter's body, you might feel a sense of shame for this thought, but repressing it can lead to inappropriate comments such as, "I'd kill for thighs as small as yours" or

"Why do you wear such tight pants? Do you always have to show off your butt?" Your daughter is likely to feel shame and discomfort about such comments.

- **Realize that your daughter's body belongs to her, and yours belongs to you:** Try not to confuse your body-image issues with your daughter's. Remember, your daughter is not an extension of you but is her own person. If you had an eating disorder as a teenager, it is okay to be concerned about this happening to your daughter, but don't rush her to a therapist and dietician if the signs of disordered eating aren't there. At the same time, if you are overweight and she is not, don't let that become an issue by trying to control her food choices. The more overbearing a parent is about her daughter's diet, the less she is able to make informed, independent, and healthy choices. Restricting a child's diet can often lead adolescent girls to overindulge as a way to have her own voice. This can produce the opposite effect of what is intended.

- **Show your daughter that it is okay to relax:** Whether you are a stay-at-home parent, a working professional, or a single parent, life's demands can cause increasing pressures on daily lifestyles. If your daughter sees you running from task to task from morning until night, she will likely behave in the same manner. Show your daughter that it's good to take time out of the day to relax. Try to schedule at least ten to fifteen minutes a day for "me" time. Announce that you are taking time for yourself by taking a bath with essential oils, drinking a cup of tea, reading a book, and just "being" instead of doing. Doing this for yourself encourages your daughter to do the same. Down time can help your daughter relax, connect with her body, and check in with how she is feeling.

- **Be aware of how you tease (especially if you are a father):** When it comes to teasing your daughter, avoid jokes that relate to her body. For example, nicknames such as "chubs" or comments made about weight or body shape can have long-lasting adverse effects on girls. Sometimes parents can tease as a way to connect with their daughter. However, teasing, as it relates to her body, can sometimes cross the line and produce shame about her body.

Impact of Media

A major factor contributing to an increase in body-image issues involves social media. Popular media depictions of airbrushed runway models are not the only culprits in creating body-image issues for today's teenage girls. According to WebMD, most teenage girls view about 180 minutes of media daily. Social media sites such as Facebook, Twitter, Instagram, and Snapchat have given rise to teens posting selfies of their "perfect" bodies for the world to see. These images can be cropped and airbrushed to add to their appeal. Also, a girl's self-esteem can be dictated by how many, or how few, likes she gets on a post. Self-criticism based on appearance can lead to a negative body image and can damage a girl's overall sense of self.

Parents play a critical role in helping their daughters have healthy relation-ships with their bodies. To start, be aware of what your daughter is up against in relation to social media. As harmful as advertising may have been when you were a teenager, it is worse now. Here are some tools to help your daughter combat the power of social media and marketers.

- **Watch television with your daughter and scrutinize commercials with her:** While viewing ads showing girls with idealized bodies, point out that viewers should be skeptical of advertisers' claims. Explain to your daughter that while it is okay to want some of the products that the advertisers are promoting, the companies are in the business of selling their wares. Each time you watch a commercial of this nature with your daughter, ask her to point out instances where advertisers use beautiful women to deceive the viewers into buying products by appealing to the subconscious desire to look like models.
- **Limit electronics time:** I know this is easier said than done. However, given the previously cited statistic regarding teenage girls being exposed to an average of three hours of media a day, this is one of the most impor-tant things you can do for your daughter. Having this much screen time prevents your daughter from having an active lifestyle in which she has opportunities for physical activities and traditional social interactions. Don't forget that your daughter is still at the age where she is internalizing the messages she observes. Many of the messages are targeted to ado-lescents. Also, you should carefully monitor your daughter's use of the

Internet in your home. Come to an agreement with all members of the family about what is acceptable. Some ideas include limiting electronics time during the week but allowing more time on the weekends, keeping the computer in a public place, monitoring computer games for violent and sexist content, and putting parental controls on the Internet.

- **Lose the magazines:** Although social media is difficult to avoid, fashion magazines—most of which emphasize weight loss, diet, and exercise—are not. The less your daughter is exposed to these magazines in the home, the better. Although she may see these images outside the home, disallowing these magazines at home sends the message that what her body looks like is not a major concern in her home.
- **Give opportunities to discuss the media:** Speak openly with your daughter about images presented in the media that depict the idealized body for women. Ask your daughter her thoughts on how women are portrayed.

Additional Tips for Preventing Body-Image Issues

- **Avoid comments about food and weight loss:** Do not comment on calories or the fat content of food in front of your daughter. Encourage others who are in your home to do the same. If you must lose weight for health reasons, do not talk about it excessively in your daughter's presence.
- **Set boundaries on "getting dressed" time:** If your daughter takes an unusual amount of time to get dressed, she may be obsessing about her appearance. It's okay to be concerned with her appearance, but if her preparation time is interfering with getting places on time, finishing chores, and completing homework, then it's reasonable to set a time limit.
- **Compliment your daughter on her many qualities:** It's nice to occasionally praise your daughter on how she looks, but it might be better to decrease the attention you give to her physical appearance and focus instead on your daughter's other qualities, such as her wit, intelligence, and athletic ability.
- **Don't cause your daughter to fear a family legacy:** If your daughter's matrilineal line tends to have women with large hips, don't tell her that she is

bound to inherit this feature. Let her come to her own conclusions about her body. Also, making frequent comments about family members' appearance shows your daughter that you notice body shape and value it excessively.

Mind-Body Connection

Another issue that arises with teenage girls who have body-image problems is their difficulty in identifying feelings. They may habitually focus on their unhappiness with their bodies in order to avoid dealing with more difficult problems. Overuse of this type of distraction is likely to occur when a teen doesn't have an alternative means to cope with distress. When this goes on for too long, it can manifest into physical symptoms such as stomach pain or headaches. Often, when a girl says she is struggling with body image, what she actually means is that she is upset about something else. It is important to help your daughter make this distinction.

Rashida came to my office after she had gone prom shopping with her mother earlier in the day. She was tearful and sullen and had difficulty catching her breath. After several minutes, she calmed down and indicated that she was upset she hadn't found a prom dress that fit her properly. She stated, "I'm such a lard. Everyone is going to laugh at me. This is going to be my worst night ever." When I probed a bit deeper, Rashida admitted that several dresses actually did fit her. After talking more, it became clear that Rashida had had a bad week. She was having problems with her best friend, and she got into an argument with her boyfriend. Rashida's way of coping with these stressors was to focus on her body, rather than her feelings, and to internalize her anger. This led to headaches and stomach pains.

Rashida's reaction is a common one. Anger and shame are more difficult and less acceptable emotions to express than pleasant feelings. Rashida was expressing her emotions in a physical way, since it was hard for her to put words to them. If you notice physical symptoms in your daughter and rule out medical conditions, this could be what is happening for her. In order to help your daughter connect with and release her emotions, you must help equip her with the coping tools to do so. The following might be useful:

- **Validate her feelings and thoughts:** If your daughter is frustrated with her body, validate her concerns instead of ignoring them. For example, if your daughter tells you, "I feel fat in this dress!" say, "I understand you have that thought," instead of disregarding her statement and moving on.

- **Help her with anger:** Give your daughter opportunities to release the energy and the painful emotions that may be underlying her body shame. Tell her it is okay to be angry and give her opportunities to express her anger in healthy ways. If expressed appropriately, anger is a useful emotion, but internalizing it can lead to self-destructive behaviors. Give her opportunities to express her anger with you, even if it feels uncomfortable at first. This will require her to experience her feelings in a healthy manner. Also, try to persuade your daughter to keep a journal of her thoughts and feelings.
- **Encourage a physical release for anger:** Teach your daughter to get into her body and release her anger. Anger can sit in the body and, if not released, lead to health problems. Buy a punching bag and allow her to hit it when she is angry. Let her throw things in the backyard if she needs to release feelings.
- **Give your daughter permission to not be happy sometimes:** Girls are socialized to feel that they must please others and put on a happy face even when they feel sad. Tell your daughter that it is okay not to smile if she is not feeling okay and that she is still loved and accepted even when she is not experiencing happy feelings.
- **Teach your daughter about deep breathing:** Give her the skills to belly breathe or meditate. Mindfulness tools will help her connect with her body and relax.

Now that you are familiar with actions to avoid, there are things you can teach your daughter to do to appreciate her body.

- Focus on what the body can do, not on how it looks.
- Ask your daughter to teach you a physical skill that you do not have.
- Help her to feel pride about her changing body.
- Connect her with positive female role models.

If you are concerned about your daughter's eating habits or recent weight loss, approach her in a relaxed way, during a nonthreatening time, such as while on a walk or in the car. Once she is relaxed, try to find an opening where you can show concern in a gentle manner. For example, instead of saying, "You are way too thin. Why aren't you eating?" try focusing on her feelings instead: "You haven't been yourself lately. Is there anything you want to talk about?" Try to ask open-ended questions and give her an opportunity to speak. If she does not want to talk at that moment, leave the topic open to be revisited. Because eating concerns elicit so much alarm, parents often have the tendency to approach this topic somewhat aggressively. Unfortunately, this may only lead to your daughter shutting down further and hiding the issue with more fervor.

Finally, if you are truly concerned that your daughter may be at risk of having an eating disorder, put together a team of specialists in the field, including a dietician, a therapist, a family-medicine doctor (who must have experience in working with eating disorders), and possibly a psychiatrist. This will be discussed in greater detail in Chapter Seven.

CHAPTER 7
Eating Disorders and Their Implications

Unfortunately, eating disorders are not uncommon in the United States and around the world. It is currently estimated that 11 percent of high-school students have been diagnosed with an eating disorder, but that only approximately 10 percent of that group seek treatment (National Association of Anorexia Nervosa and Associated Disorders 2017). More concerning is the fact that people with eating disorders have the highest mortality rate of any mental illness among people of all ages.

Eating disorders are complex mental-health issues and can be difficult to understand. They usually do not occur in isolation, but rather along with such other mental-health problems as mood disorders, generalized and more specific anxiety disorders, bipolar disorders, and difficulties that result from trauma.

Eating disorders entail much more than frequent dieting in order to lose weight. They characterize extremes in eating behaviors, from total abstinence to bingeing on up to thousands of calories per day. They affect families and friends, as the teen often plans her entire day around when and what she will eat, as well as how she will carry out her exercise or purging regimen.

In many cases, someone with an eating disorder may have begun the process by eating slightly smaller or larger amounts of food, eventually finding that her eating issues are spiraling out of control. Extreme concern about body weight is often evidence of an eating disorder. Types of eating disorders include anorexia nervosa, bulimia nervosa, and binge-eating disorder.

Having a daughter with an eating disorder can be a major stressor for the family. It is a life-threatening mental-health and medical issue that affects the entire family system. It has a major impact on the way in which the family interacts, including preparing food, going out, and going on or missing out on vacations.

Causes of Eating Disorders

Although there may not be a single cause for an eating disorder, certain factors commonly play a role in developing such problems. Included are a genetic predisposition, co-occurring mental-health issues, family discord, and low self-esteem. Additionally, the media's emphasis on thinness likely plays a major role in why teens want to be thinner. Certain sports, such as gymnastics and dancing, where body size and low weight are emphasized, may also contribute to eating disorders.

In some cases, the individual with the eating disorder may not be the only person in the family with either an eating disorder, eating concerns, or mental-health issues. Generational patterns may exist prior to the onset of the eating disorder, as there may be a history of mood disorders, control issues, and perfectionism.

Types of Eating Disorders
Anorexia Nervosa

People with anorexia nervosa (more commonly referred to as anorexia) have an extreme fear of gaining weight, coupled with a distorted view of their body size. They commonly believe that their body is much larger than it actually is. They often restrict the calories they consume in order to lose weight or to maintain an extremely low body weight. Teens may fast, purge, and exercise excessively. Losing weight can become an obsession, and teens may engage in additional practices to assist in weight loss. These include using laxatives, consuming excessive caffeine, and abusing medications. The following are medical symptoms of anorexia:

- Cessation of, or failure to develop, menstruation
- Difficulty sleeping
- Bouts of dizziness or even fainting on occasion
- Discoloration of the fingers, which may appear bluish
- Thinning or losing hair
- Growth of fine, soft hair that covers the body (known as *lanugo*)
- Constipation
- Intolerance of cold

- Irregular heart rhythms
- Low blood pressure
- Dehydration
- Osteoporosis
- Hair damage

Red Flags for Anorexia

Often those with anorexia disguise their weight loss, making it difficult for others to recognize that there is an issue. The following are signs that there might be a problem:

- Engaging in unusual rituals with food (e.g., cutting food into small pieces, mixing food with an excessive amount of condiments, etc.)
- Chewing and spitting out food
- Wearing loose, large clothing
- Skipping meals
- Making excuses for not eating
- Eating only an extremely limited variety of foods
- Weighing or measuring oneself constantly

Anorexia Case

Carly, age fourteen, was in treatment after her family began to suspect, during the previous year, that she had an eating disorder. Her family-medicine doctor confirmed that Carly had, in fact, lost thirty pounds in the past twelve months, had stopped menstruating, and had passed out during a gymnastics meet due to an electrolyte imbalance. Her mother described, with exasperation, how awful it was watching Carly "lose her hair" and expose her bones when she lifted her shirt. Carly rolled her eyes and said that her mother was exaggerating and that she "looked fine." Her mother further indicated that medical tests revealed that Carly had significant health issues. Carly's doctor recommended that she enter a residential treatment facility.

By the time of our first meeting, Carly had completed three months of treatment at the facility and regained twenty of the thirty pounds. Carly was still not allowed to return to gymnastics until she could show that she was able to maintain her weight.

In meeting alone with Carly, however, it became clear to me that despite all the problems anorexia had caused her, she had every intention of losing weight again.

Carly told me she had been a popular girl in elementary school. She said that things came easily to her and that she was a star gymnast and student. However, after she began getting her period, she had more difficulty keeping the weight off. Her struggle increased as she progressed to more competitive gymnastics. She concluded that if she lost some weight, she would give herself more of an edge competitively.

The weight came off faster than she anticipated. Once she began losing weight, she explained, she started to feel her self-esteem increase and thought, "Just a few more pounds will do it." Carly explained that she derived a high from watching the numbers on the scale decrease. She also noticed that the weight loss made her feel a sense of control in other areas of her life. If she got a low grade on a test, but her weight was down, she still felt in control. If her parents argued, she could not control the conflict, but she felt that she could control how little she ate that night.

In speaking with Carly, it became clear that her recent hospitalization might have temporarily improved her medical condition but that her underlying psychological issues were not yet resolved. Her perfectionist tendencies put her at great risk, as she relied on her anorexia to cope with daily stressors. The treatment team would need to work with Carly and her family to help her continue gaining weight, but she would also need to develop positive coping tools for dealing with ongoing pressures. This would allow Carly to feel a sense of control without relying on weight loss to achieve this state.

Bulimia Nervosa

Bulimia nervosa (more commonly referred to as bulimia) is characterized by cycles of binge eating, following by compensatory behaviors to undo the effects of the binge. People with bulimia typically binge in private on a large number of calories, ranging from hundreds to thousands, and then purge the calories. After the binge, purging can take the form of self-induced vomiting or abuse of laxatives, diuretics, or enemas. Often someone may restrict calories throughout the day and then binge and purge, never really getting a full meal. The following are medical complications of bulimia:

- Dehydration from excessive purging, which can lead to kidney failure
- Low potassium
- Heart problems

- Severe tooth decay
- Gum disease
- Absent or irregular periods
- Digestive problems and irregular bowel movements
- Drug or alcohol abuse

Red Flags for Bulimia

There is a great deal of shame associated with bulimic behaviors, and it is often difficult for someone with bulimia to discuss what she is experiencing or to ask for help. If someone has just binged and purged, she is often embarrassed about the incident and may try to keep this information private. However, getting this person help is crucial. If you observe the following behaviors in your daughter, there might be a problem worthy of further exploration:

- Evidence of missing food
- Candy or food wrappers in trash cans
- The presence or smell of vomit
- Withdrawal from her usual activities or friends
- Diet-like behaviors
- Continued exercise despite injury
- Use of a bathroom immediately following a meal
- Use of laxatives, diuretics, or enemas

Bulimia Nervosa Case

Charlotte, age seventeen, had been a client of mine since she was fourteen. When we first met, Charlotte had just been placed with her fourth foster family. She had been restricting her caloric intake since she was twelve. Charlotte had a horrific history of trauma from the time she was a young child. She restricted in order to be so skinny that other people would find her unattractive, thus avoiding the unwanted sexual advances she had encountered earlier in her life.

Eventually, restriction became too difficult to maintain, as she began a cycle of bingeing and purging. For Charlotte, food became a comfort to her whenever memories of past trauma were elicited. However, she felt shame about the amount of food she had ingested and had an instant need to regurgitate it. Charlotte explained that vomiting was a release for her—like letting go of all the bad feelings and pent-up tensions she was carrying inside her.

Charlotte's most recent foster family had been trying to legally adopt her after meeting her when she was fourteen. She tried to scare them off by showing them that she was bulimic, but the foster parents persisted by showing her loving care and setting her up with a treatment team. Charlotte still not did not allow her potential parents completely into her life, because she feared they would eventually abandon her. She had learned from her traumatic, inconsistent, and chaotic past that people are not to be trusted and that numbing and hiding from feelings are the best ways to cope with them. The one constant in her life had always been food.

Charlotte's treatment underwent many ups and downs. She went in and out of treatment facilities, and once even made a suicide attempt. As this book is being written, Charlotte is slowly learning to express her needs and set limits with others. There have been periods of time when she has not engaged in her bulimic patterns. However, in times of high stress, she has returned to her bulimic behaviors. Charlotte's team and foster parents are hopeful that, in time, Charlotte will begin to love herself and not resort to self-destructive ways to get her needs met.

Binge-Eating Disorder

Binge eating describes behaviors in which someone binges on large amounts of food regularly but does not compensate for the intake of food through any form of purging behaviors. Bingeing has major medical implications, including:

- High blood pressure
- Gallbladder disease
- High cholesterol
- Heart disease
- Type II diabetes

Red Flags for Binge-Eating Disorder

- Eating large quantities of food
- Eating rapidly without a break
- Eating rapidly during binge episodes

- Hoarding food
- Frequently dieting without weight loss
- Eating alone
- Hiding empty food containers
- Spending large amounts of money on food

Who Is at Risk for Eating Disorders?

Eating disorders frequently appear during the teen years or young adulthood. However, they may also surface later in life, or even in childhood. Research indicates that the earlier the eating disorder is detected and treated, the greater the chance of recovery. This is why it is essential that your daughter be treated as soon as possible if you discover that she has an eating disorder.

Effects of Eating Disorders

In addition to the physical effects of eating disorders, the emotional pain may be a great burden on teens and their loved ones. When someone develops an eating disorder, it often becomes the focus of her life, and it is difficult for her to generate sufficient energy for other important activities. Planning or avoiding meals takes a great deal of effort, and it is common for teens with eating disorders to hide some of their behaviors from public view in order to avoid social embarrassment.

Tips for Helping Your Daughter

It can be very challenging to contend with an eating disorder. If you confront your daughter, she may initially be very defensive, deny that she has a problem, and refuse treatment. If she agrees, the best approach may be to take her to an outside professional, such as her family doctor or a therapist, who has expertise in eating disorders. It is sometimes easier for a person to acknowledge and discuss a problem with an objective third party than with a family member. An experienced professional can help confront the denial and present the issue in a way that may be more palatable to your daughter.

Many of the tips for dealing with eating disorders are similar to those provided for body-image problems, but there are several additions:

- **Look at your own relationship with food and body image:** You have a major influence on your daughter. Consider how you approach food and body weight and how this may affect your daughter.
- **Avoid threats:** As frustrating as it may be to see your daughter engage in unhealthy behaviors, threats or offensive language will only make things worse. Try to understand how your daughter is feeling, and determine how you can support her when she is struggling with these serious problems.
- **Gently describe the consequences of your daughter's behavior to her:** If your daughter engages in behaviors that are dangerous to her health, let her know what the likely consequences are, but do it a kind and caring manner.
- **Take time for self-care:** This is an extremely stressful time for you, but do not constantly blame yourself. Many circumstances are beyond your control. Find the time to care for yourself and get your own assistance if necessary.

In addition to your support, it is essential that your daughter receive treatment for her eating disorder. A professional who has expertise with eating disorders can help assess the severity of the eating disorder and make recommendations for the level of care that is necessary. The following treatment team should be in place and in contact with one another throughout the course of treatment:

- **Therapist:** Individual and group therapy can help your daughter explore underlying issues and provide alternative coping tools. Family therapy can help improve communication in the family and increase support within the family system.
- **Dietician:** Registered dieticians can help your daughter develop a meal plan. Dieticians can also help educate your daughter about healthy eating habits and teach her which food groups should be included in her diet. They can help determine when meal plans need to be increased or decreased and can make recommendations about how frequently and intensively your daughter should exercise.
- **Psychiatrist:** Psychiatrists are often part of the treatment team, since eating disorders often co-occur with other mental-health problems. Medication may be effective for decreasing anxiety. For example, some

studies show that medications such as Prozac have been successful in treating bulimia.

- **Physician:** A family-medicine doctor should conduct continual weight checks and run medical tests to determine whether your daughter's lab results are within normal limits. If they are not, this is often a sign to the team that a revision in the treatment plan may be necessary.
- **Support group:** Eating-disorder support groups may decrease isolation and reduce any shame your daughter is experiencing. She also might learn coping skills from her interactions with other group members. Support groups also exist for family members.

Members of the treatment team should be in frequent contact with one another, since a holistic approach is most effective in providing continuity of care.

If your daughter does, in fact, need a higher level of care than an outpatient treatment team can provide, she may require one of the following:

- **Residential/inpatient treatment:** Residential or hospital-based care may be required when there are severe physical or behavioral problems. It may be necessary for someone who is resistant to treatment or has medical complications that require a physician's supervision. It may also be necessary if there is continued weight loss, malnourishment, suicidality, or other serious medical psychiatric concerns.
- **Partial hospitalization:** Partial hospitalization or day treatment allows a person to live at home but receive intensive treatment five to seven days a week for approximately six to seven hours per day. It usually includes a medical, therapeutic, and nutritional component.
- **Intensive outpatient:** Intensive outpatient care also allows a person to live at home and attend school. Treatment is typically three to five days per week for three to four hours per day, often in the evenings.

Self-Care and Patience: The Key Ingredients for Success

Because dealing with your daughter's eating disorder will be trying for you, it is essential that parents and caregivers find assistance for themselves. This may be a support group, a therapist, or a caring friend. Recovery will have many bumps along the way, and at times, the eating disorder may cause you to feel that a stranger has taken the place of your daughter.

It is also important not to blame yourself for what is happening and to be patient with your daughter as well. Recovery will not happen overnight, and it is helpful to recognize and appreciate, both individually and as a family, even the smallest of accomplishments. Continue to be positive with your daughter and with yourself, and remember—taking care of yourself will help set a positive example for your daughter.

CHAPTER 8
Dating Concerns, Sexual Activity, and Dating Violence

Although the dating world can be a new and exciting arena for them, teenage girls face a variety of issues when they confront it for the first time. These include coming to terms with their sexuality, making the choice about whether or not to be sexually active, and defining how far they are willing and comfortable to move in these areas. They are also faced with the issue of sexually transmitted diseases (STDs) and pregnancy prevention, as well as concerns about sexual assault.

Parents must also come to terms with the fact that their daughters are maturing and becoming sexual human beings. Some parents have considerable anxiety about their daughters' dating. It signifies that their daughters are growing up and are entering adulthood. It is helpful for parents to explore their own attitudes toward relationships and sex. Teens who feel that they can talk to their parents about dating and sex are more likely to ask them questions and less likely to engage in high-risk sexual behaviors.

Therefore, if you feel uncomfortable discussing these topics with your daughter, admit this to her. You can say something like, "It is hard for me to talk about sex, since I never talked about this with my own parents, but I am here to help you if you have questions. We can try to problem solve together."

Today's World of Dating: It's Not How It Used to Be
Parents should familiarize themselves with the modern world of dating. Dating among teenagers is not what it used to be. The image of a boy calling a girl on the

house phone to ask her to go to a movie on Saturday night is long gone. If a girl does go out, it is typically in a group setting, not on a solo date. It is likely that you will never have a phone conversation with some of your daughter's friends, since most of their communication occurs through their personal technological devices. Also, don't expect to meet your daughter's friends immediately, since it is likely that if someone does swing by the house, the person will first send your daughter a quick text asking her to come outside. Dating today can also mean that your daughter will chat with someone on one of many social media platforms and may change her status to "in a relationship."

Just because there are new realities in the dating world, it does not mean that you have to stay out of the picture. You have a right to meet your daughter's friends and to be comfortable that she is keeping the right company. Be sure to talk to your daughter regularly about her dating relationships and agree on some ground rules, such as weekday and weekend curfews.

Also, it is important not to push teens into dating relationships, especially when they are only in middle school. Even comments such as "you will be a heartbreaker" or "all the boys will fall at your feet" can sexualize girls at an early age. Research indicates that the earlier teens start dating, the sooner they become sexually active.

Think about Your Own Dating Experiences

Prior to talking to your daughter about dating, consider your own experiences with relationships. What kind of model have you been for your daughter? For example, be aware of how you resolve conflicts and whether this manner of interaction is a healthy example for your daughter. Although your own interactions do not have to be perfect, it is important to be aware of what template your daughter has for her relationships.

What do you believe you have modeled in terms of what a relationship should look like for your daughter?

_____

_____

_____

_____

_____

It is possible that your daughter has had some type of dating relationship by this point, since 35 percent of teenagers between thirteen and eighteen report having either been in a relationship, gone out with someone, or "fooled around with" someone (PEW Research Center 2015). Given that they are novices in this arena, teenage girls are vulnerable to intense and sometimes unhealthy relationships. Provide opportunities for your daughter to speak with you about her relationships, and let her know that you are available to talk at any time.

Talking to Your Daughter about Dating

Although your daughter might act as though she is sophisticated in the dating scene, it is likely that she will be confused and anxious at this stage of life. A teenage girl needs to know her value *independently of dating* and to recognize her own uniqueness and strengths. Many times, a teenage girl will date in order to gain the approval of her peers. It is essential that parents talk to their teenagers about what it means to date and to be in a caring relationship. They must teach their daughters that people who are interested in each other must put in the time and effort required to make the process work.

Think about your own first experiences in the dating world and what supports you may have needed from a caring adult. How would you define a healthy relationship?

_____

_____

_____

_____

_____

_____

Helping Your Teenager Understand What Love Is

Molly's parents called me one winter day in the middle of a snowstorm, requesting an emergency session. During the weekend, they found text exchanges on Molly's phone that were sexual in nature and involved a schoolmate with whom the parents were unfamiliar. Several weeks earlier, Molly asked to go on birth-control pills, stating that she was having cramps during her period and that she wanted the pill to help her with her cramping and "moods."

Molly's mother said to her, "Now it all makes sense. I can't believe this is happening, and you didn't even tell us. Who have you become? We didn't raise you to be like this." Molly sat there with her head down, clearly embarrassed.

Molly's dad was visibly upset as he sat with his fists clenched. He stated, in a controlled whisper, "Sweetie, I wish you had come to us. We aren't angry with you. We just wish you had been more open with us. We don't even know this guy!"

Molly asked her parents to leave the room so she could speak with me individually. When I asked her what was going on, she expressed a mix of emotions—anger at having been discovered and confronted by her parents, but elation when she told me about a boy named Jed, with whom she had initially communicated online. I admit, I was a bit shocked as well that this was the boy she was referring to, since it seemed that their relationship developed very quickly. She must have sensed my surprise, because she stated, "I swear to you, this is real; we are so in love."

Teenagers often state that they feel their parents do not take their relationships seriously. Although teens may claim to be "in love," and parents may ridicule this assertion, saying they are "too young to feel this way," it is essential for parents to recognize that their daughter's feelings are still real. While it is important to recognize and validate their feelings, parents can also help to differentiate between infatuation, lust, and love—all of which their daughters may be experiencing. Explain to your daughter that:

- **Infatuation** means an intense, short-lived admiration for someone that is all-consuming, with an obsessive wave of emotion.
- **Lust** is a very strong sexual desire or an altered state of consciousness initiated by the urge to procreate.
- **Love** is an intense feeling of deep affection that takes time to develop. It is not about neediness, and it takes time for trust and love to develop in a relationship.

Teenagers' Views on Sex

Teenagers are having sex early, and sex is spoken about in many arenas quite openly. Just as there has been a tendency for adults to engage in casual sex, teenagers are following the trend and doing the same. Even more notable in my experiences with teens is that many do not regard oral sex as having actual *sex*. For many, their attitude often is that it is no big deal. With both parents frequently working outside the home, and with a large number of single parents, teenagers are using their unsupervised time as an opportunity to have various forms of sex.

Although it may be tempting to skip the topic of sex with your daughter, it is in your daughter's best interest to have conversations with her on this topic multiple times. Ideally, your teen should get the information from a trusted adult such as a parent, rather than relying on someone you don't know. Make it into a conversation, rather than a lecture. You can weigh the pros and cons of abstaining versus being sexually active, if your daughter is willing to have such discussions.

Conversations about sex should go beyond its physical aspects, so that teenagers understand that sex involves care, trust, and connection. If your daughter understands the emotional aspects of physical relationships and feels comfortable talking with you about this topic, she is in a better place to make informed choices for herself. These conversations should also include discussions about how she can protect herself from pregnancy and STDs.

Are Teenagers Ready to Be Sexually Intimate?

Two months after my initial encounter with Molly and her family, I sat with her again. A forlorn-looking young girl, she appeared much younger than age sixteen, and it dawned on me that despite how old she acted at times, Molly was, in fact, just a kid. Molly was tearful and stated that she felt "heartbroken." Jed broke up with her, stating that he felt that things were moving too fast and getting too serious. He told her that he felt he wasn't ready to be in such a serious relationship at his age, and that although he still loved her, he could only be friends with her right now. Between bursts of tears, Molly stated, "What is worse is that I saw him commenting on another girl's Instagram posts. I think he likes her, and that's why he isn't with me anymore. I honestly just want to die."

The reality is that teenagers are not going to abstain from dating and sexual activity just because the adults around them tell them to do so. However, one of the concerning issues about teens engaging in close personal relationships so young is that they are not necessarily emotionally mature enough to be in an intimate relationship. In the above scenario, Molly fell in love hard and fast. Being physically intimate hastened this experience. Although this can happen with adults as well, teenagers are not necessarily prepared to handle the emotional intensity of such relationships, particularly if they end quickly, as in the case above. Although she said she wanted to die, luckily Molly was not suicidal, but she did struggle for much of the remainder of the school year with depression and self-doubt.

Teens and STDs

A further concern related to teenagers having sex is the risk of pregnancy and STDs.

Breanna and her boyfriend, Tre, had been together for over a year. He was a senior, and she was a junior in high school. They became sexually active after being together for nine months and had intercourse after her junior prom. When I asked Breanna about how things were going, she said that she was happy with him and that he treated her really well. She said, "It's not like we're going to get married or anything. He's going to college next year, so we're going to see other people then, but when he comes home, we'll still hang out."

I asked, "Breanna, are you still using protection?" She told me, "I'm on the pill now, so it's so much better. He doesn't really like the way condoms feel, and we definitely don't want a baby. I mean, Tre still sometimes uses a condom, but we don't have to worry about it as much...what's the big deal? He's my first, and he's only slept with one other girl before me. I'm sure he will use condoms when he's away...it's not like he's stupid or anything. Gosh, you and my parents get so uptight."

AIDS and other STDs are a reality. Teenagers need to get messages at school, from their parents, and from each other that if they are going to engage in sexual activity, they must use protection.

As her parent, you have every right to communicate to your daughter your expectations about dating and sex. However, communication should be done in a thoughtful and caring manner. Parents need to be available to talk things through, to answer questions, and to help their daughters navigate what can be a difficult and confusing time for them. Here are some tips for helping your daughter get through this phase of life, while also making expectations clear:

- **Communicate your values:** Let your daughter know what your values are with respect to relationships and intimacy. Although your daughter may not adopt all your recommendations, it is still important that she know where you stand on these issues.
- **Use gender-neutral pronouns when referring to anyone whom your daughter may be interested:** If your daughter is experimenting with her sexuality, or if you are not sure if she is lesbian, gay, bisexual, transgender, or queer (LGBTQ), do not use words like "him," but just say "they." Doing so will demonstrate your acceptance, thus allowing her the safety to tell you if she is, in fact, LGBTQ.

- **Don't feel pressure to be an expert:** If you do not know all the answers to your daughter's questions about dating or sex, don't worry. Knowledge is less important than the way you respond. You can research responses to questions at a later time. Just be open, and try not to overreact if your daughter asks you a question, so you can explore the answer together. It's probably hard enough for her to ask.

- **Have your daughter invite her love interest over for a casual meal or dessert:** This will give you an idea of how they interact with each other and whether or not their relationship appears healthy. Inviting the love interest over will also help your daughter discuss the relationship, if she chooses.

- **Give your daughter age-appropriate autonomy, but ask her to check in with you while she is out:** This can be through a simple text halfway through the evening that will let you know she is okay. Although your daughter might protest when you make this request, it might also make her feel cared about.

- **Be a role model:** If you are in a relationship, your actions—even more than your words—are essential to teaching your daughter what it means to be in a good relationship. Be in tune with what messages you are conveying about your own relationships.

- **Talk to your daughter about risks:** No matter how often she has been told, you can still tell her the risks of unplanned pregnancies and STDs. Give her the tools to protect herself, and provide her with the opportunity to ask you questions.

- **Provide your daughter with relevant literature:** If she does not wish to speak with you about pregnancy and STD prevention, provide her with books and articles on these topics so she can read material on her own. This may avoid an uncomfortable conversation while still getting the job done. Contact your daughter's doctor's office or school, or go online for literature.

- **Speak to your daughter respectfully:** If you broach sexual topics in a nonconfrontational, nonthreatening manner, your daughter will be more likely to open up to you and share her thoughts, feelings, and concerns. She will feel understood rather than judged.

- **Be direct:** If you think your teen might be embarking on a sexual relationship, it's okay to ask her a straightforward question such as "What's happening with the two of you physically?" Remember: be sure to continually have conversations with your daughter about dating and sex. Teenagers name their parents as the number-one factor in their decisions about sex. These conversations can delay their decision to be physically intimate and positively influence their decision to use protection consistently.

- **Stay calm:** Although you may be alarmed if you learn that your daughter is sexually active, it is important to stay calm. If you say something out of anger, you may regret it later and shut down further conversations with your daughter on this topic. Being able to talk to your daughter in a calm way can have a significant impact on her ability to construct healthy relationships and to have safe sex.

Teen Dating Concerns

Teen dating violence is an area that is rarely spoken of, despite its prevalence. Shockingly, one in three adolescent girls in the United States has experienced physical, sexual, emotional, or verbal abuse from a dating partner. This exceeds rates of other types of youth violence. Furthermore, girls and young women between the ages of sixteen and twenty-four experience the highest rate of intimate-partner violence—almost triple the national average (Love Is Respect 2016).

Half of teenagers in relationships report having been controlled, threatened, and coerced by their boyfriend or girlfriend. As previously stated, teens actually *want* to talk about relationships with their parents. Sixty-two percent say they wish they could talk more openly with their parents about relationships (Jewish Women International 2014). If teens *do* talk to their parents about relationships, it is seldom about dating abuse. Adults are more likely to talk to teens about drugs, alcohol, and sex than they are about dating abuse, and they are not aware of how large of an issue teen dating violence actually is. Parents usually have little awareness that their children are even at risk.

Intimate-Partner Abuse among Teenagers

Abuse comes in many forms. It can be physical, emotional, financial, technological/digital, and/or sexual. It is important to remember that a relationship may be abusive even if there is no physical violence. Most abusive relationships do not start out with physical violence. The important factor to note is that abuse is a pattern of power and control of one person over another person. It spans all socio-economic backgrounds and cultures.

Digital abuse is a type of emotional abuse perpetrated online. The perpetrator can be in constant contact with the victim, demanding check-ins and tracking where the victim is at all times. An abuser may also demand and share private or sexual images and messages or can hack into an adolescent's e-mail or social-media accounts. Abuse often escalates over time.

Cycle of Abuse

Abuse occurs in cycles. There are times when a relationship may seem positive, as it was in the beginning. However, tension builds and is often followed by a concerning incident. There is then what is known as the honeymoon phase, which is when the abuser apologizes and promises to change. However, the abuse will likely return and may become more severe. Victims of teen dating violence are more likely to

- struggle with schoolwork;
- experience depression, anxiety, and other mental-health issues;
- engage in risky behaviors that involve drugs and alcohol;
- attempt suicide;
- engage in physical disputes;
- isolate themselves from friends and family; or
- have an unplanned pregnancy.

Abusive behaviors are likely to escalate over time. If a teen stays in an abusive relationship into the college years and beyond, the abuse will probably become even more toxic. Stepping in immediately can break the cycle and protect teens from a potential lifetime of abuse.

Red Flags

Seeing the red flags of an abusive teen relationship can be difficult for an outsider. Teens are often private about, and protective of, their relationships. If they are not talking about their relationships, and the adults in their lives do not have access to their digital networks, such as their phones, Instagram, Facebook, and the like, it is difficult to know what is going on in their daughters' relationships. Nevertheless, it is possible to observe some signs that your daughter is in an abusive relationship:

- Excessive texting, calling, or other contact may mean that an abuser is trying to dominate the victim's attention and control how she spends her time. This may initially be difficult to identify, since teens often text; notice, however, your daughter's posture and affect when she is texting. Does she seem tense? Is she trying too hard to justify her actions or appear apologetic to you about the person she is communicating with? If so, these are warning signs that are worth discussing.
- Tense, dramatic conversations laced with arguments.
- Unequal power dynamics in the conversation, such as her partner answering questions for your daughter or telling her what to do or how to dress.
- Intense exchanges of affection such as "I love you" early in the relationship.
- Excessive jealousy on the part of the partner.
- Less time spent with her friends or engaged in the activities she formerly enjoyed.
- Constant put-downs from partner—calls her "stupid" or "unlovable."
- Impulsive behavior such as reckless driving by the partner.
- Threats by partner to self-injure if your daughter leaves. If your daughter is being told that her partner will self-injure if she leaves, this is a **huge red flag** and a major manipulation tool. What she is really being told is that "I will hurt *you* if you leave me." Regardless, no one is responsible for anyone else's actions, and it is her choice to leave a relationship, despite any threat imposed on your daughter.
- Unfounded accusations that she is flirting or cheating.

One of the main problems is that a novice in relationships often labels behaviors such as jealousy and possessiveness as being "sweet." Your daughter might think, "Look how much my partner likes me." The trouble with this is she may miss the warning signs of an unhealthy relationship. Parents and caregivers of teen girls must continue to have conversations with them early on, both before dating starts and while they are dating, to inform them of the warning signs and to help them understand what healthy relationships entail.

Signs of Dating Abuse

Teen dating is often kept hidden for a variety of reasons. Often, teens do not even realize they are in an abusive relationship, since they are inexperienced with dating relationships and may regard the one they are in as the norm. They are happy about their independence and may feel more accepted by peers because they are in a relationship. Additionally, they often have very romanticized views on what love is supposed to look like. Here are some signs that your daughter might be in an abusive relationship:

- Inexplicable marks or bruises
- Wearing long-sleeved clothing during warm weather
- Withdrawn, depressed, or anxious behavior that is not her baseline mood
- Withdrawal from extracurricular activities or other interests
- Different clothing style; for example, wearing looser clothing because her partner doesn't like her to show off her body or attract the attention of others
- Scholastic changes such as truancy or declining grades
- Anxiety if she can't text or call her partner right back because he or she might get upset

How to Respond

First and foremost, if your teen is in immediate danger and the abuse is, in fact, physical, then immediate action is required. This entails potentially calling the police, alerting the school, or filing a protective order. (Legal options related to protective orders vary by state.) Additionally, it is important to reach out to a professional to help create a safety plan to protect your daughter. Safety plans often entail the following:

- Changing passwords and getting new accounts on digital devices
- Blocking perpetrators from contact on social media
- Switching methods and routes of transportation to and from school
- Alerting school staff, neighbors, and other responsible adults about potential dangers
- Changing your daughter's school locker or locker code
- Documenting the abuse in a journal

- Keeping spare change, a phone, and a phone charger in your daughter's possession at all times
- Considering who your daughter should call if stranded and keeping those numbers on her at all times

For less severe but still concerning forms of mistreatment, the following guidelines might be useful:

- **Use caring statements:** When approaching the topic with a teen, parents and other caregivers should open with statements such as "I care about you and want you to be happy. I believe that you deserve to be in a relationship where you are valued and treated with kindness and respect."
- **Explain the difference between unhealthy relationships and abusive relationships:** In an unhealthy relationship, the couple may communicate poorly, disappoint each other, or otherwise not get along well. The individuals might be a poor match, have different priorities, or not meet each other's needs. In an abusive relationship, however, one partner deliberately gains and maintains power and control over the victim.
- **Explain what dating abuse means:** Many teens do not know what teen dating abuse even means. They may be familiar with terms such as *domestic violence*, but they may not be aware that there is a term to describe the relationship they are in. Putting a name to dating abuse and defining the term will help your daughter understand that she is not alone.
- **Don't interrogate your daughter:** If your teen opens up to you, realize that it is difficult for her to come forward. Don't put her on the spot by demanding detailed information or proof of what happened. Also, don't interrogate your daughter by questioning or judging her choices or behaviors. Sentiments such as "I told you he wasn't good for you" or "You never listen" are not useful and make your teen defensive.
- **Take her seriously:** Value your daughter's experiences and feelings. Don't minimize what she is experiencing. It is important to believe her. If she tells you that a well-respected boy, one you know well, is the perpetrator, and you find this hard to imagine, do not dismiss the possibility this this is true. Note that dating abuse does not discriminate on the basis of familiarity.
- **Let your daughter know it is not her fault:** Often the abuser uses manipulation and control to convince the victim that the abuse is her

fault and that if only she could change, she would not be in this position. Remind your daughter that she *never* deserves to be abused, the abuse is *never* her fault, and she deserves to be in a healthy, caring relationship.

- **Provide your daughter with options, rather than giving her orders:** Giving alternatives will allow your daughter to feel that she now has control over a situation she once felt was out of her control. By giving orders, you can make her feel further coerced. Providing options will allow her to feel empowered and to have ownership in her choices.

- **Offer your daughter the option of speaking with someone who is unbiased:** Your daughter may feel more comfortable speaking to a therapist, a school counselor, or a religious leader. If the abuse is unusually serious, seeking professional help is highly recommended. Professionals who are trained to deal with abuse know the available resources and have the ability to work with victims and their families. Try not to take the engagement of professional help as a personal rejection. It is sometimes easier to talk to someone removed from the situation. Your daughter may be excessively concerned about worrying you. Your family will be in good hands if you are working with a trusted professional who has experience with this type of problem.

- **Try not to be judgmental:** This is not a time for lecturing or giving your opinions on sex, technology use, and dating. Yes, your values are valid; however, it is important for your daughter not to feel judged for her actions, which can further perpetuate her sense of shame. Keep the focus on support and how you can help your teen.

- **Help your daughter to engage with support systems:** If your daughter was formerly isolated from friends, social outlets, and enjoyable activities, encourage her to reconnect. If you suspect abuse but your daughter has not told you about it, keep in mind that the majority of teens who do report abuse first relate it to a peer, not an adult. Additionally, friends are more likely to witness the abuse than are adults.

- **Express love and concern:** Be sure to let your teen know you are concerned for her happiness and safety and are available to talk whenever she needs you.

- **Be specific about which behaviors concern you:** If you are worried that your daughter is not spending time with her friends, don't say, "I don't like Connor. He's so possessive." Instead, try "I noticed you don't spend as much time with Janie, Eric, and Sarah anymore. I know you mentioned that Connor likes to have you all to himself. I'm concerned because I know how much you like being with your friends too. Is everything okay?"

- **Describe to your daughter what a healthy relationship looks like:** If you are in a healthy relationship, or can reference a couple who is, use that as a starting point. Use examples. A caring partner
  - respects your autonomy;
  - trusts you and believes you;
  - supports your interests, goals, and dreams;
  - cares about you and your feelings;
  - respects your boundaries;
  - values your opinion;
  - does not pressure you to do anything that is out of your comfort zone; and
  - does not punish you or hurt you.
- **Encourage your daughter to trust her instincts:** If something does not feel right to her, tell her to trust her gut feelings. You will likely need to have this conversation more than once. Leaving an abusive relationship is a difficult process and can even be dangerous.
- **Be prepared to have the conversation regularly:** After the first conversation, be prepared to revisit the conversation repeatedly once your daughter has had time to process what you have discussed. It also shows your daughter that you believe the issue is serious and that you care.
- **Review the options:** Due to the dynamics of abuse, the victim may become accustomed to being told what to do. Help empower your daughter to make a decision, but review the options with her.
- **Limit contact:** As her parent, you can impose limits on technology use and require that your daughter turn her locked cell phone in to you before she goes to sleep at night.

Helping a Teen End an Abusive Relationship

Ending a relationship, even an abusive one, can be very difficult for a teen. Even when abuse is involved, there are times when the abuser is very loving, making it difficult to end the relationship. Your daughter might hope that her abuser will change their ways, as they have likely promised. Be in tune to the fact that ending an abusive relationship is not the same as ending a healthy one. Your daughter's partner may not accept the breakup or respect her boundaries. Abuse through social media adds a complicated dimension to ending a relationship. Often break-ups are texted and posted all over social media. Pictures and statements about each party can exacerbate the situation to the point where one party is humiliated. Additionally, the abuse survivor may bear a great deal of guilt about ending the relationship and fear for her partner's safety and well-being. As the girl's parent, you need to realize that ending the relationship is often the most dangerous time. Bear in mind that if too much pressure is placed on the teen to break up, it is possible that she will carry out the relationship in secret and cease to communicate with you about it.

Here are some tips to help your daughter get through a breakup if she's in an abusive relationship:

- **Encourage your teen to not break up in person if she does not feel safe:** If she does decide to do it in person, have her do it in a public place where you or other trusted adults are nearby.
- **Trust her instincts:** Although mentioned earlier, this is important to reiterate. If your daughter does not feel that things will be safe for her, they are not—trust her! Safety planning or going to the authorities might be necessary.
- **Encourage her to call 911 if necessary:** If your daughter is in danger, make a safety plan, and encourage her to call 911 if she feels unsafe.
- **Visit the Love Is Respect website (http://www.loveisrespect.org) for an interactive guide to safety planning.**

CHAPTER 9
Separation, Divorce, and Blended-Family Issues

Separation and divorce present difficult and sensitive challenges for all family members. Depending on the circumstances, divorce can affect the children involved in various ways. The process and its aftermath affect teens differently than younger children or adult children.

No family is "good" at divorcing; however, the way in which the issues are handled is crucial to your teenager's well-being. For some girls, the breakup of a family may signify the end of childhood. As described in chapter 2, the teenage years are a time of transition from being a child to forming a personal identity separate from one's family. A major developmental task for all teenage girls during this phase of life is to gain some independence and prove that they can become self-sufficient. When a divorce coincides with this stage, a teen may suspend the process of separating and instead take care of one or both parents' needs. Alternately, a teen may speed the process of separation by further rebelling and detaching completely. During this period, it may be difficult to determine whether the changes you notice in your daughter are due to normal developmental issues, a result of the breakup, or both.

Unfortunately, there is no simple answer to the questions above. However, if your daughter had a strong sense of self and a relationship with one or both parents prior to the separation, then things will likely improve over time. Most important, though, is how the coparenting relationship is handled with the original parents and any stepparents in the picture.

When Separation is Difficult

Miranda and her father sat in my office. Miranda refused to speak to or look at her father. Instead, she sat in silence and looked at me. Finally, she spoke. "When can I get out of this room with this loser? When is my mom coming to get me?"

Miranda's father, Owen, was clearly very frustrated. He said, "Miranda, I know you are upset with me, and you have a right to be angry, but this is between your mom and me. I am here to talk to you today about how we can work through this and how to help you work through stuff. I can't wait for you to see my new place and have you start coming over. You will love it!"

Miranda heaved an exasperated sigh. "Seriously! If you fucking think I am coming near your new home, you have to be out of your mind. I can't fucking stand you, and I'll never forgive you. I don't even know why I let you come here, after you slept with that other woman for like who knows how long, and who knows what else you did...I want nothing to do with you, and now I know I never want to get married either, thanks to you. Now leave my therapy time, or I'll go."

Miranda's father looked shocked. "Miranda, like I said, this is between your mom and me. How do you even know about that...whatever? That's not important now. I just want to talk to you about us."

A furious Miranda got up and stated, "There is no us. What don't you get? You made your choice when you decided to ruin the family. Bye!" Miranda proceeded to storm out of my office.

Teens' Reactions to Divorce

While no two teens react in exactly the same manner, there are some common themes that teens experience when their parents separate. Often children feel shame, despite the fact that many of their friends have gone through a similar situation. Also, the shift in family dynamics can cause a change in their identities, which may feel like a betrayal. Additionally, they may attach themselves to one parent over another, or they may blame themselves for their parents' divorce. They may also think about their own future relationships and become more cynical about their prospects of having a partner.

The difficult feelings children experience when coping with their parents' divorce can be mitigated when parents forge a congenial relationship in accordance with the best interests of the children. When parents argue in front of the children, it is particularly difficult for teenagers, who often feel they have to be loyal to one parent over another—a terrible choice for children to have to make.

Another concern with which teens must contend is how the divorce will affect their own lives. They are often quick to ask with whom they will live, how their finances will be affected, and if the time spent going back and forth will interfere with their social lives. These are real concerns for your daughter. Take the time to talk through these issues with her, hear each concern, and address them when you are able.

For many teens, handling the many difficult facets of life in this stage is stressful as it is. They must deal with school, extracurricular activities, and social life. A change such as a divorce can further burden your child and cause significant anxiety. Traveling between homes, adjusting to a second home, and coping with the loss of her family as she once knew it, can be exhausting. Therefore, providing as much consistency and as little stress as possible is essential. Here are some communication tips for you and your ex-partner that should help ease the adjustment process.

- **Tell your daughter together:** When telling her that you have made the decision to separate, it is best if both parents tell her together. This shows your daughter, from the start, that you are both there to support her and that one parent is not solely in control of the situation; *both* are. It gives her the message that both parents will work on this together and that coparenting should follow a similar trajectory in each home.
- **Give your daughter information but not all the details:** Kids want to be given information and told the truth about the situation with their parents, but most do not want to hear all the details. Spare your daughter the particulars of why you and your ex-partner are separating, and focus on the changes that will affect her.
- **Learn to coparent:** Despite the problems you may have faced as a couple, coparenting is probably the most important thing you can do for your daughter. Teenagers from divorced situations who grow up in homes where both parents provide loving environments and common boundaries can thrive as well as children in nuclear families. Teens are most likely to succeed when their parents work together, have regular communication, and enforce consistent rules.

- **Don't make your daughter take sides:** Despite what issues you may be facing with your ex-partner, do your best not to involve your daughter. Let her feel free and comfortable to interact with the other parent. Make sure she knows she does not have to choose sides or loyalties. Your daughter is not responsible for either parent's happiness, and it is most beneficial to her development to have a relationship with both parents.

- **Try to shield your daughter from unnecessary issues:** Unless she was somehow involved in the demise of your relationship, such as being a victim of domestic abuse, your daughter should not be privy to the details of your breakup. If you are constantly rehashing the events that led to the breakup, do so without her present. Do not allow her to get unnecessarily involved, even if she asks for information. Your daughter should not be a sounding board, and issues should not be discussed when she is in earshot. Children's resiliency is strengthened, and they are less stressed, when there is less obvious conflict between their parents.

- **Do not make your daughter a messenger:** If you want information conveyed to your ex-partner, do it yourself. This returns us to the point on coparenting. Find ways to communicate about sensitive topics that do not unnecessarily involve your daughter.

- **Allow both parents to be present:** Work out your differences so that both parents can attend events such as school gatherings, teacher conferences, and sporting activities. It is helpful for your daughter to still have the security of both parents being present and supportive. It is ideal that the parents sit together at events, if they are able to get along. If not, at least having both parents in attendance will show your daughter that you are still able to be present for her and to give her support.

- **Don't put down your ex-partner:** Be aware of criticizing your former partner in front of your daughter. She will likely hold on to any comments your make, even if they seem insubstantial to you. Be aware of your body language, such as rolled eyes, dirty looks, nasty gazes, sighs, and other nonverbal cues when talking about your ex-partner. Your daughter is likely very sensitive to these cues.

- **Try not to fish for the details of her visit with your ex-partner:** Although you may be interested in hearing about your daughter's weekend away with your former partner, don't give her the third degree. Show interest by asking how the weekend went, but asking your daughter for too many details may cause her to feel she is being used to spy on the other parent.

- **Seek support for your family:** Separating is really difficult to do alone. Seek the support of a family or individual therapist to assist you with the transition. You and your ex-partner can also seek a professional to work on coparenting issues, if you are having difficulty.

Managing Split Time

Teens, in particular, are concerned with the logistics of their postseparation environments. They are often interested in knowing what changes will be put into place and how the changes will affect their lives. They are anxious to know when they will see which parent, how they will see their friends, how they will get their schoolwork done, and whether they will be able to carry on with their regular activities. It is advisable for your daughter to have a say in the specifics of her schedule. You may not be able to grant all her wishes, but it is important that she have input. Your daughter is also likely to be concerned about the changes in the family's financial situation and how they will affect her life.

Teenagers fare best when they continue to have relationships and spend time with both parents, regardless of where they spend the majority of their time. Research indicates that children have higher self-esteem, better grades, and fewer tendencies toward mental-health problems when they are regularly involved with both parents, provided there is not current abuse or a history of abuse.

Both parents must work together on setting limits. It is important to achieve a united front, since raising teens is itself challenging, and the breakup of the parental unit can present opportunities for teenagers to manipulate situations. If your daughter is aware that her parents are not communicating, she may take advantage of it. Both parties must continue to discuss and agree on rules and have a working relationship to set limits on such issues as curfews, parties, and schoolwork.

Parents must also bear in mind that adolescence is a time of separation (refer to chapter 2) and that teenagers need to foster their independence. The split of your relationship can cause a delay in this process if your daughter feels that she must step in and help one or both parents. Additionally, girls may be more drawn toward their same-sex parent (that is, their mothers), and fathers may naturally feel that they are losing their relationship with their daughters.

To further complicate this, the time that teenage girls do spend with their parents might decrease the time they spend with their friends. Parents can best serve their daughters by not personalizing their daughters' desires to meet their own needs. Their daughters are already likely feeling torn about how to distribute their time between family, friends, and activities.

Navigating Split Time Between Homes

Amanda, age sixteen, was the daughter of Caren and Jim, who had divorced four years earlier. Amanda's parents were coparenting remarkably well and got along with each other, despite a few minor disagreements. Amanda was doing well in school, had an active social life, and was the captain of her ice-hockey team. I had seen her regularly during the divorce, but now she only came in periodically for check-ins. Amanda's mother remarried two years prior, and now Amanda had a stepfather and younger stepsister, whom she adored. Her biological sister was away at college. Her father was single. Amanda spent half her time with her father and slept at his house every Saturday night.

Amanda related that although she was faring well since the divorce, she was struggling with guilt. She indicated that during the time she was with her father, she could sense that he was somewhat lonely, and although he claimed he was doing well, he was overjoyed with her company. This made her feel bad when she went out with her friends on weekend nights. Amanda had been making excuses to stay home on Saturday nights, telling her father that she felt sick or just had too much homework. Amanda's father encouraged her to go out, but it was hard for her to leave him on the nights she stayed at his house. To add to this, Amanda did not look forward to her time with her father. She felt more at home at her mother's house, which was livelier than her father's. Also, she liked being around another female (that is, her mother) but didn't have the heart to tell her father that she wanted to spend more time with her mother.

In this case, it was clear that Amanda's parents were doing the important work of coparenting. However, as is very common, Amanda struggled with the time she spent with one parent. Both parents were supportive, but they did not communicate that it was okay for Amanda to still be a kid and take care of her own needs. Although it's important to follow a schedule, what is more important is the quality of time spent with each parent. Amanda helped resolve this problem by asking her dad to do something interesting with her before she went out with her friends.

This mitigated her guilt about leaving the house on the nights she spent with her dad and gave her dad some quality time with his daughter. Allowing kids to separate and continue this aspect of their development is essential to their growth.

Children are also more likely to succeed when both parents have a positive influence on, and participate in, their lives. If there is a parent who has less time with a child, this parent can still be involved with activities such as sports and homework and can provide emotional support. Here are some additional tips for managing the shared time:

- **Stay in touch:** Maintain your relationship with your daughter by staying in touch with her on the days she is not with you. Call her to check in, or have a set time to talk. Stay in touch throughout the day through text or e-mail to let your daughter know you are thinking about her and that you are interested and involved in her life even when you are not physically with her.
- **Try to keep residences nearby:** It is ideal when both parents live in the same township or part of the city. This way, your daughter can maintain her friendships in either neighborhood, and transportation to school and activities will be facilitated. This is a win-win for both parents and teens, since it will increase the amount of time together, and it simplifies everyone's lives.

Stability and support are important qualities to provide all teens but particularly following a separation. For example, when you tell your daughter that you will visit on a given day, pick her up, or have her on a set day, follow through. If you are going to be late, let her know. Teens, like children of all ages, need consistency at all times, but particularly when going through a transition. Not showing up may send a message that you do not care or that you do not want to be involved. Your daughter needs to know that even though your relationship with her other parent has changed, your relationship with *her* will be consistent. Here are additional ways to continue providing dependability and support:

- **Be present:** Parents who are in the midst of separation may have difficulty being present for their own children, particularly in the first year after the breakup. Be sure your daughter knows that you are available and that she can ask you questions and voice concerns, even though this is a difficult time in your life. Parental presence from both mother and father can ease the transition and the troubling emotions their children are experiencing.

- **Keep lines of communication open:** After you have had the initial conversation explaining that you are separating, continue to communicate with your daughter about the changes taking place. Open dialogue can create an atmosphere where your daughter is unafraid to ask questions and voice her concerns.
- **Set a calm tone in the home:** Try to maintain a mellow, positive attitude in the home. It is okay for your daughter to see you upset sometimes, but try to keep the overall atmosphere one of calmness and minimal drama. With all the changes going on, it will be helpful for your daughter to have a safe, peaceful place to help her feel grounded.
- **Be in tune with any signs of distressed behaviors:** Be aware of signs of depression, changes in sleeping or eating habits, or lack of interest in the activities in which your daughter normally engages. If you notice any of these signs, observe whether this is a pattern, and be sure to check in with her about them.
- **Ask others in your daughter's life about her:** Check in with other adults in your daughter's life about how they think she is coping. She may act one way at home and another way in a different environment. Check with her school staff, coaches, and friends' parents, as well as family members, to learn their impressions of how your daughter is faring with respect to the divorce.
- **Continue to set limits:** Don't give your daughter everything she wants to compensate for feeling guilty about the divorce or to win her favor over the other parent. Work with your ex-partner to set limits, and try to keep the rules and boundaries consistent in both homes.
- **Allow your daughter time to transition when moving from one house to another:** It may take some time for your daughter to adjust after switching from one home to the next. If she does not seem like her usual self at first, give her some time to readjust before checking in with her.
- **Take care of yourself:** Get support for yourself, and do not expect your teen to take care of you emotionally. Even if your daughter is a good listener, it is not her job to support you during this time. Get your own support so that you are not projecting your issues onto her.

- **Seek out a teen support group:** Many schools and communities have groups for teens who are going through a divorce. It might be helpful for your daughter to join a group to connect with other teens who are having similar experiences.

Remarriage and Blended Families

If you make the decision to remarry, be aware that things may not always go smoothly, at least initially. It is wise to prepare for a period of transition. Changes to a family structure require adjustment and patience. It can take quite some time for all involved family members to be comfortable with the new situation and function healthily together. This is a period of major change.

Although the new couple might be very excited about the new arrangement, do not be surprised if your daughter does not share in your enthusiasm. It is natural for her to be apprehensive about these changes and their effect on her relationship with you. She will also likely be concerned about her relationship with her future stepparent and any stepsiblings in the new family. A great deal of care and thought is necessary when planning for this transition. It is best to move slowly when making big changes and to keep an open dialogue. Making too many changes at one time can be unsettling. It is best to wait at least two years or more after the parental breakup before creating more major changes.

Adjusting to Change is not Always Easy

Carolina and her mother, Maria, were sitting in my waiting area. Maria was bright eyed and full of life, which was a relief to see, since the previous two years had been quite difficult for her. Maria and Carolina's father separated two years earlier, and the family went through a difficult transition. One year ago, Maria started dating again, and she was engaged to be married in two months.

When Maria saw me, she stood up, gave me a huge smile, and said, "Well, I'm off to a wedding-dress fitting. Two more months until the big day!"

Carolina looked up from her iPhone and mumbled, "Aren't you coming in for part of the session, Mom, like you usually do?"

Maria looked up and said, "I wish I could, honey, but I already made this appointment, but I'll be back soon. It's just right down the road. Text me when you need me to pick you up. Love you!"

Carolina shuffled into my office. She looked at me and said, "Well, at least some-one is happy about this marriage."

I was a bit confused and said, "I thought you liked your mom's boyfriend."

Carolina said, "Yeah, as a boyfriend. I didn't expect him to be moving into my home already. He takes up so much space, and his little kids, when they come over, are so loud that I can't get any homework done. Plus, she makes these big meals for him, and he eats them like a pig. It's like I'm not even there. Oh, and did I mention that he asked me if I wanted to call him Papa? I was like, seriously, are you kidding? I have a dad, buddy. By the way, did you see how quickly she bolted out of here? She used to beg to come into these sessions!"

Parents' and their daughter's needs are very different during this time of tran-sition. As a parent, it is a wonderful feeling to meet someone and eventually make a long-term commitment after experiencing the loss of a relationship. For many adults, it can signify exciting new beginnings. For your daughter, however, it can represent quite the opposite. No matter how much time has elapsed since the split with your ex-partner, your daughter may still be struggling with the grief related to the loss of her family as she knew it. Bear in mind that she is a teenage girl and is going through her own set of concerns and changes during this period of her life. This, coupled with the changes in her family structure, can be unsettling. A new relationship may also represent the loss of the dream of her parents reuniting, since that is often the enduring hope of children of divorce. Your daughter may also be wondering where her place is in your life and whether your new partner has replaced her. Your daughter may also be worried that if she forms a relation-ship with her stepmother, for example, then she is not being loyal to her biological mother. She may also want to know about the role this new person will play in terms of discipline and rules in the new blended family.

Managing Rules with Blended Families

Courtney was seventeen and attended a boarding school a half hour from her father's home during the week. Because the school was closer to her father, she spent the weekends with him, her stepmother, her stepbrother (age seven), and her step-sister (age ten). Courtney's father and stepmother had been living together for four months.

Courtney described a difficult encounter with her stepmother. "So I came home for the weekend and couldn't wait to go out on Friday night with my friends, who

I've missed while away. We'd been talking about this party all week, and I was sort of like the guest of honor, since I'd been away for so long. Anyway, I didn't get home till like 1:00 a.m., because we were having so much fun, and we kind of lost track of time. Besides, now that I'm in boarding school, it's sort of like being in college, and we always hang out late on weekends. Even when I lived at home, my dad never really gave me a curfew. He just trusts me and makes me promise to never get in the car with someone under the influence. So I come in, and my stepmother is standing in the doorway, looking like she is ready to pounce on me. I mean, we're talking like psycho-style here. She starts screaming at me and telling me how irresponsible I am and asks me what drugs I smoked—I don't even get high! Then she starts talking about how she won't get any sleep, how tired she will be tomorrow because of me, and that I'll be a bad influence on her precious kids. So then my dad comes down and starts fighting with her, so they go into their room in private. Next thing I know, she's apologizing to me, and it's like 2:30 a.m., so I'm like, whatever, I'm going to sleep. Seriously, they need to get it together. I don't know what's going on or what rules are in place anymore. It just makes me not even want to come home. Next time I think I'll stay at Emma's house. At least her parents are normal."

As is clear in the scenario above, relationships and rules are difficult to navigate in newly blended families. Even if you and your partner have agreed on ways to run the newly formed families, there is likely to be confusion both initially and along the way. Here are some tips for when the time comes to introduce a new partner and possibly that person's children into your daughter's life:

- **Move slowly:** Wait to introduce your daughter to your new partner until you have communicated as a couple that you plan to be serious. Don't have your partner step in as an enforcer of rules right away. Let your daughter develop a relationship with your new partner by spending small increments of time with her or him, so she can develop a sense of comfort.
- **Negotiate, communicate, and renegotiate the roles:** Before remarrying, discuss with your partner how you both plan to parent. Be aware that you may need to make some adjustments to your styles of parenting. At some point, your partner will be required to step in as an enforcer of household rules. Talk to each other about what this will look like, and troubleshoot to see how the new arrangement is working out. If it seems to need tweaking, continue to converse about the roles, and try another

tack if necessary. If you are combining homes, where children from both parents will be living together, it is all the more important to discuss the rules. You must come to a consensus on making the rules consistent and specifying who is responsible for carrying out the rules of discipline.

- **Maintain connection with your daughter:** Make time for just the two of you, or the two of you and her siblings. Your daughter needs to feel that she is a part of your life and that she is not being replaced with her stepparent or stepsiblings.

- **Prioritize your relationship with your daughter:** Be sure that your partner understands that the transition may take time for your daughter and that she is still a priority. This is not to undermine the importance of the relationship with your new partner, but your partner needs to understand that your daughter's needs are still of utmost importance to you.

- **Set realistic expectations:** Don't expect your daughter and your new partner to get along perfectly all at once. Likewise, if you are becoming a stepparent, don't assume that the relationship will develop immediately, all in *Brady-Bunch* style. Although you may be expending a great deal of love and energy on making this relationship work out, the chemistry isn't always there. Just because you have a close connection with your partner, it doesn't mean that your daughter will. She may have trouble getting used to the idea of one or more new people living in her home. Take it one day at a time.

Although I have not painted a fairy-tale picture of this transition, and you may be filled with a mixture of emotions—including sadness, anger, and guilt—when you divorce, it is important to recognize that positive things may very well come from the changes your family is undergoing. For example, I have heard parents say, "I feel much closer to my children now that my troubled marriage has ended" or "I now feel much more relaxed when I walk in the house." Teenagers of divorce eventually realize that their parents needed to move in different directions and that there will be some benefits from the new family structure. Continue to take care of yourself through this process. The hope is that you will feel optimistic about the future and that one day you may see this transition as just a bump in the road to a better state for your family. The process of divorce is never easy, but the outcome might be beneficial for all parties.

CHAPTER 10

Drugs, Alcohol, and Other Risk-Taking Activities

A dolescence is a time for exploration. For many, this time of life is associated with an increase in risk-taking behaviors. These behaviors include activities such as smoking, drinking, using drugs, having unprotected sex, driving recklessly, fighting, being truant, overusing video games, and gambling. These behaviors are not new phenomena; they have been prevalent for decades. The question we should *not* be asking is "What's wrong with kids these days?" This way of thinking will not help parents deal effectively with problems. A more useful approach is to ask, "What risky behaviors are currently facing teens, and what can parents do about them?"

In order to understand teens and the risks they take, we must understand the world in which they live. Keep in mind that adolescents are focused on establishing their identities, fitting in with their peers, measuring up to others, and experimenting with new behaviors.

Taking risks is a normal part of life and might be a healthy endeavor. Taking some risks can help your daughter develop into a confident, diversified individual who is aware of her capabilities. Some risks, however, are dangerous. It is important that your daughter be able to differentiate between healthy and unhealthy risks.

- *Healthy risk taking* entails engaging in an activity where there is the potential for failure but for which the consequences are largely safe. Examples include competing in sports, engaging in travel adventures, and meeting new people. Other examples include getting on stage, asking someone out, or auditioning for a show. The important point is that these activities satisfy your daughter's need to push boundaries, and the downside consequences are usually minimal.

- *Unhealthy risk taking* includes behaviors that can have grave consequences, including reckless driving, texting and driving, bingeing and purging, and engaging in other impulsive behaviors. The desire to be accepted by peers often exacerbates these behaviors. Often teens engage in behaviors such as running red lights only when their peers are in the car with them.

Although parents and other adults often interpret risk-taking behaviors as acts of rebellion, it is a normal and healthy part of development for your daughter to experiment with some risky behaviors. Due to changing expectations and adolescent brain development, teen girls often engage in risky behaviors. If you are aware of these behaviors and have concerns, talk to your daughter about them. You can help her identify the pros and cons of engaging in the behaviors. If she has her mind set on a certain behavior, consider ways to reduce the risk involved. Ask her questions such as why the activity is important to her at this time, or whether there is anything she could do that is less risky. If the activity is intolerably risky, then you must explain to her that the behavior is unacceptable. Then choose the appropriate limit. The three problems of particular concern that will be addressed in this chapter are driving recklessly, engaging in substance abuse, and playing video games to excess.

Driving

Mechanically operating a vehicle is a fairly simple activity to master with some practice and supervision. For teens, however, it can be a challenge to learn to drive safely. A lack of maturity and changes taking place in the frontal lobes of the brain can make the multiple tasks required while driving difficult. Your daughter may appear ready for the task of independent driving when she is in the car with only you. She might be challenged, however, when she drives with other teens and experiences chattering friends, blasting music, buzzing cell phones, and changing traffic lights. The combination of peer pressure, incomplete brain development, and inexperience at the wheel can result in risky driving.

Tips to Encourage Safe Driving

- **Model safe driving:** Model safe driving well before your daughter gets behind the wheel. Do not text and drive. Be aware of engaging in road rage, running red lights, and cutting off or cursing at other drivers while you are in the presence of your daughter. Make a document called Ground Rules for Road Safety. Come up with a list of parameters of what is expected of your daughter once she gets behind the wheel. The specifics might include not using alcohol when driving, always wearing a seat belt, not texting and driving, following curfews, and agreeing to have no more than a set number of passengers in the car.

- **Recognize positive driving behaviors:** Your daughter has a great need for independence at this stage. Initially, you may limit her driving by not allowing her to drive with friends in the car. You can gradually allow her to have a friend or two in the car after she reliably exhibits positive driving behaviors.

Substance Abuse

Whether used as a medication, for recreation, or to gain social acceptance, drugs and alcohol alter the chemistry of the brain and markedly affect behavior. Due to peer pressure, teens are already more susceptible to situations and risk factors that would put them into contact with drugs and alcohol. Characteristics of the adolescent brain increase its likelihood of being attracted to and responsive to some substances that activate the cerebral reward system. Once cells in the reward system of the brain are activated, the neurotransmitter dopamine is released, producing a feeling of pleasure sometimes approaching euphoria and increasing the likelihood that teens will continue to use these substances. In addition, repeated use of some substances can cause the brain to become tolerant of the substance, causing teens to use dangerously high levels to attain a previously achieved psychological state. More concerning is the fact that neuroscientists speculate that teens are more likely to become addicted to illicit substances than are adults because the pleasure centers of the brain develop more rapidly than the part of the brain that governs decision making and impulse control.

Additionally, the lack of development of the frontal lobes makes resisting temptation more difficult and causes teens to experiment with other dangerous substances. This, combined with peer pressure and the desire to fit in, makes teens likely targets for substance abuse. This is not meant to excuse teens for engaging in substance abuse; however, this information can be useful to parents when implementing preventative and corrective interventions with their children. These strategies will be discussed later in the chapter.

The two most common forms of substances are alcohol and recreational drugs.

Alcohol

Of all the dangerous substances, alcohol is the most commonly abused. The average age at which teen boys first try alcohol is eleven; for teen girls, it is thirteen.

Teenage girls turn to alcohol for a variety of reasons, many of which are the same for their male counterparts: psychological issues, biological predisposition, family stressors, curiosity, and peer pressure. The use of alcohol may ease the process of fitting in with peers, since it can act as a social lubricant. This topic will also be discussed in greater detail later in this chapter.

Whatever the reason a teenage girl drinks, the consequences can have a major impact on her welfare. For some, drinking can delay the onset of puberty. Additionally, teenage girls are more likely to engage in unprotected sex while under the influence of alcohol—increasing the chances of pregnancy and STDs—and drinking by teen girls puts them at a greater risk for sexual assault or date rape.

The younger a person is when she starts drinking, the more likely she is to develop a problem associated with alcohol. Alcohol is major factor in car crashes, and teenage girls who drink are at greater risk for attempting suicide than are girls who do not drink. Additionally, excessive drinking can lead to the use of other drugs, such a marijuana, LSD, and cocaine.

Binge drinking, which entails consuming four or more drinks in one sitting for females, can lead to passing out or to a complete blackout. Peers and family may not view this type of drinking as problematic, since it has become common for teens and college students to binge drink on weekends. However, this behavior can result in alcohol poisoning, sexual assault, bodily injury, drunk driving, and falling behind in school. If binge drinking is not dealt with effectively, it can become life threatening.

Drugs

It may come as no surprise that in 2015, 31 percent of tenth graders and 45 percent of twelfth-graders had used marijuana (Child Trends 2017). Notably, the marijuana of today is significantly more potent than earlier versions. This means that users are exposed to stronger strains of the drug than was previously true. Studies on animals have indicated that marijuana use can decrease intellectual, social, and athletic development and can possibly put adolescents at risk for more serious psychiatric disorders, such as schizophrenia, later in life, according to the National Institute on Drug Abuse (National Institute on Drug Abuse 2016).

The use of pain medication, or narcotics, such as Percocet, Vicodin, and OxyContin has been on the rise among teens for the past decade. Although their primary purpose is to blunt pain, they activate the opiate receptors in the brain and can produce euphoria. They are highly addictive and can kill users with only one dose.

Benzodiazepines, such as Xanax, Ativan, and Klonopin, are prescribed by physicians to treat anxiety, panic attacks, and sleep problems. However, teens may abuse these medications to get high or feel more relaxed. Withdrawal from benzodiazepines can take a long time and can be life threatening if not done under medical supervision.

Cold medicines, such as NyQuil and Robitussin, are easy to obtain and are commonly abused by teens as a means of getting high. The chemical dextromethorphan (DXM) is the potent ingredient that, depending on the dose, can cause users to get high or even hallucinate.

Ritalin, Adderall, and other stimulants used to treat attention deficit and hyperactivity disorder (ADHD) are being abused by teens in order to stay up late, lose weight, and achieve a speed rush. Students with a prescription sometimes sell the medication to their friends. If this medication is used as prescribed, it does not produce the dangerous effect that it does when abused.

Ecstasy, or MDMA, known as the "love drug," is touted to make users feel warm, sociable, open, and connected. In reality, though, it is a synthetic drug similar to the hallucinogenic mescaline. Ecstasy interferes with the serotonin levels in the brain and ultimately causes brain cells to die off permanently. It can also impede the body's ability to regulate temperature, leading to hypothermia.

Methamphetamine, or crystal meth, is the most addictive drug available today. It provides its users with an abundance of energy, culminating in a sudden crash that can cause severe depression and even the urge to commit suicide.

Cocaine makes users feel on top of the world and full of energy, and it can also produce weight loss, since it may act as an appetite suppressant. The long-term health effects of cocaine use can include irritability, restlessness, anxiety and paranoia, paranoid psychosis (that is, loss of touch with reality and auditory hallucinations), and increased risk of exposure to HIV and other diseases. Teens are at a high risk for developing an addiction to cocaine.

Bear in mind that not all drug and alcohol use is a sign of addiction or pathology. Teenagers *do* experiment with drugs and alcohol, particularly at high-school parties. Labeling all use as addiction can lead to more intrusive treatments than are necessary.

So, you may ask, how can you determine whether your daughter has a substance-abuse problem? One major factor that plays into substance addiction is genetics. If there is a family history of substance addiction, your daughter has a much higher risk of becoming addicted.

Substance Use in Families

Jackie, fourteen, sat as far as possible from her mother, Katiya. Jackie had a sullen expression and seemed not the slightest bit concerned with her distraught mother's ramblings. Katiya was speaking frenetically about having found marijuana, bottles of vodka, and Percocet tablets in Jackie's drawer. "Her father and I feel that she is out of control, and she never listens."

Jackie retorted, "I just hate you guys. You don't care about me now. All you care and talk about is what will happen when I am grown up, and where I will go to college. You make me go to sleep at nine o'clock, and you still check my phone and iPad. You are all over me all the time. You just aren't normal."

I asked Jackie to take a break and sit in the waiting area, and she obliged, stating, "Anything to get away from her!" As I spoke to Katiya, I learned that both of Katiya's parents were alcoholics, and Katiya and Jackie's father were fearful of Jackie becoming one as well. Katiya told me that she and Jackie's father were both first-generation Russian immigrants. She explained that her own parents were not very present in her life and that she grew up in an impoverished village. Katiya described her parents as being abusive, that they placed no limits on her, and she was free to come and go as she pleased. Katiya's father was also raised by alcoholic parents and left home when he was sixteen.

Jackie's parents made the decision to raise their children with controls and surveillance, but it was clear that there were few displays of love and affection. Although Jackie was at risk for addiction, she was also angry about her parents' control and the lack of privacy they afforded her and was challenging the limits she encountered.

During the next session, when I spoke to Jackie alone, she told me that she resented the limits and restrictions that her parents placed on her. When I asked her about the substance abuse, she told me she liked the way the alcohol made her feel and that being with the kids who used these substances was a nice break from being with her uptight family. She said she didn't actually like the drugs she tried, but that drinking distracted her from the anger inside her.

Throughout the course of treatment, we worked toward the goals of the parents showing more love and affection to Jackie, loosening some of their constraints, educating her about the risks of substance abuse, and finding other outlets for her risk-taking needs, such as rock climbing and playing in a band.

Reasons a Teen May Engage in Substance Abuse

In order to understand teen substance abuse, it is important to be aware of some of the factors leading to this problem.

- **Observation of others:** If your daughter sees her friends smoking weed at a party, she may regard this is an acceptable part of teen culture and assume that her friends expect her to behave in a similar manner.
- **Thrill seeking:** As previously discussed, your daughter may be looking for new, dangerous experiences with peers.
- **Depression/anxiety:** Drugs can be used to self-medicate. If your daughter is feeling anxious or depressed, or she's lacking in self-esteem, her state of mind can be altered since the drug temporarily helps her escape her negative feelings and emotions.
- **Enhanced social status:** Using drugs may up a girl's social status and make her appear more cool or popular with the "in" crowd.
- **Weight loss:** Drugs such as caffeine, amphetamines, and stimulants can lead to weight loss. Some teens who are prescribed stimulants for ADHD have been known to share or sell their prescriptions to peers, who will buy them in order to help them lose weight. When taken without a medical need or in higher doses than prescribed, stimulants may act to suppress appetite.
- **Misinformation:** Many teens are highly misinformed about the dangers of substance abuse. For example, many teens do not know the risks involved with trying heroin "only once." Additionally, many teens are also under the impression that prescription drugs are much less lethal than street drugs.

What Are the Signs of Substance Abuse?

It is also important to be aware of signs that your daughter may be using dangerous substances. These signs include, but are not limited to the following:

- Changes in personality
- Verbally or physically abusive behavior toward others
- Possession of drug paraphernalia
- The odor of drugs on her person (for example, solvent smell of inhalants, marijuana smell)
- Changes in friends
- Missing items or money
- Increased drowsiness or sleeping
- Secrecy in activities or placing the bedroom off limits to family members
- Withdrawal, isolation from friends, and decreased interaction with friends and activities
- Failing grades at school

Tips for Preventing Substance Abuse

- **Create an open dialogue:** Be proactive in bringing up the topic of substance abuse. Ensure that your daughter knows that no matter how difficult things get, or how much pressure builds, she can come to you for support or questions.
- **Avoid lectures:** Ask your daughter her views on substance abuse. Solicit her opinion on the topic, and observe her verbal and nonverbal responses. Talking about substance use will not tempt your daughter to engage in it. It will let you know her views and help you to understand what to expect from her.
- **Give your daughter the tools to say no:** Role-play with your daughter situations in which she may have to verbally set boundaries when faced with peer pressure. Play out scenarios in which other people challenge your daughter to use drugs.
- **Provide your daughter with an out:** Let your daughter know that if she does not feel comfortable in a situation, she can always contact you. Make sure she understands that you will pick her up to get her out of a dangerous or uncomfortable situation no matter what time of night and that no questions will be asked at the time.
- **Know your daughter's friends:** If her friends are using drugs, she is more likely to use them also. Get to know her friends and her friends' parents.

- **Know your daughter's whereabouts:** Keep track of where your daughter is. When she says she is going to a party, find out if there will be adult supervision and if alcohol will be accessible.
- **Set a good example:** If you abuse drugs and alcohol, you are setting an example that this behavior is acceptable behavior for your daughter.
- **Set limits and expectations:** Let your daughter know what is expected of her and what the consequences of substance abuse are. Teens are less likely to use drugs if they know the adults strongly oppose it.

Video Games

Boys and girls are equally attracted to video games. Playing video games is not an example of substance abuse, but doing so inappropriately and excessively can lead to behavioral disorders that interfere with important aspects of a teen's development. Repeated exposure to violent video games has the effect of desensitizing users to violence (Huesmann 2007 4). In addition to increasing aggressive behavior, teens who play video games excessively are more likely to engage in high-risk behaviors such as alcohol use, drug abuse, and unprotected sex (Dartmouth News 2014). Brain development is affected by video-game usage. Playing video games may cause teens to act inappropriately. Since teens do not have fully developed frontal lobe control, after viewing a violent game they have less capacity than an adult to suppress the urge to act violently when they are angry. Video games are not going to disappear; the industry will continue to increase its efforts to market them to teens. Therefore, it is not realistic to completely eliminate them from your daughter's life. However, here are some ways to manage your daughter's video-game usage and decrease the negative impact they may have on her development:

- **Know what she is playing:** Discuss with your daughter what games she is playing. Ask her to observe the behavior of the characters, how they handle conflict, and how the videos depict women.
- **Be aware of the rating of the video game:** The Entertainment Software Rating Board assigns rating information so that parents can make informed decisions about what games are acceptable in the home.
- **Set limits:** Set restrictions on the frequency and amount of time your daughter plays video games. The less time she spends on the games, the

less impact they will have on her behavior. Let your daughter know that she cannot play games until her schoolwork is complete.

- **Discuss consequences:** Discuss with your daughter the consequences depicted in video games. Show the irony of the common portrayal of violent behavior without penalties.
- **Play a game with her:** While playing with her, discuss conflict resolution and alternatives to violent and cruel behavior.
- **Select nonviolent games:** If your daughter is adamant about playing video games, try to encourage ones that do not involve violence. Encourage her to play games that involve strategy, teamwork, or problem-solving skills.
- **Be aware of interactive games:** Some games involve interactions with strangers online. Teach your daughter to be cautious and to recognize whether she is communicating with a stranger. Monitor these conversations.

Ways to Reduce Dangerous Risk Taking

Do not fret over this stage of your daughter's life. There is much to be enjoyed and gained during this phase of life, and generations have survived situations they thought were intractable. This is a critical time for your daughter to build confidence and to learn how to manage risk while capitalizing on some positive opportunities she will encounter. You do not want your daughter to hide in a closet during these years! Here are some strategies that may help your daughter improve her judgment during this challenging and exciting stage of life:

- **Help your daughter delay the onset of drinking:** Much research points to the benefits of this suggestion (Parenting Strategies 2017). The earlier in life that kids start drinking, the greater the chance for developing dependence. Teens who drink a lot, often come from homes where the parents are heavy drinkers. Be aware of your own health-related habits.
- **Provide information:** Many teens lack information on the risks associated with drugs and alcohol. Provide your daughter with the knowledge and tools for dealing with substance abuse.
- **Help your daughter assess risk:** Look for ways to teach your daughter to identify unhealthy risks and their consequences.

- **Devise ground rules:** All caregivers can come up with ground rules for what is expected of teens. Try to do this in collaboration with your daughter. Figure out what the distinction is between safe experimentation and dangerous behavior.
- **Be aware of your daughter's whereabouts:** Keep an eye on your daughter. Try to have dinners together in order to establish a steady, consistent time that you are connected. Be aware of your daughter's daily routine and her whereabouts.
- **Pay attention to your daughter, and spend time together:** Sometimes healthy experimentation can evolve into unhealthy risk taking as a way to get attention from parents who are too busy to notice what their daughters are doing. Make an effort to spend quality time with your daughter, and be fully present when you are together.
- **Communicate:** Keep open communication lines with your daughter. If she is forthcoming with you about some of her concerning behaviors, try to not use judgmental language. For example, if your daughter opens up and tells you that she drinks to fit in, don't say, "You can't go to parties anymore if you drink." Instead, talk to her about why she feels she must drink. Try to open the dialogue about what is going on with her, without jumping right into lecture mode.
- **Be a role model:** If you run red lights or get behind the wheel after having several drinks with dinner, consider whether this is the example you wish to set for your daughter.
- **Give your daughter decision-making tools:** Involve your daughter in making important family decisions, such as where to vacation, what to eat for dinner, and how to spend the weekend. This will give her the tools to rely on her own judgment, plan ahead, and build confidence in her choices.
- **Help your daughter build self-control:** Your daughter may be engaged in texting and playing video games at the expense of schoolwork or family time. Instead of completely banning these activities, help her to allocate her time properly.

CHAPTER 11

Challenges of Technology and Social Media

While there is much buzz about the manner in which technology and screen time affect toddlers, it is no news that technology use, particularly social media, has taken partial control of the lives of teens. Due to the convenience of phones, teens are able be online daily, and they likely to spend more time interacting in the virtual world than in the real world. According to a Kaiser Family Foundation study, kids spend an average of seven hours and thirty-eight minutes a day connected to some type of electronic device (2010 2). How does this play out at home? When spending time with your daughter, you might notice that:

- She can text or swipe at record speed.
- You seldom see her face, since she is usually looking down at her phone.
- You constantly hear text tones or vibrations.
- If she leaves her phone somewhere, or her phone is taken away from her, she behaves as if she has lost a body part.
- You feel like a fifth wheel when you are with your daughter, and she is connected to her electronics.

Digital Natives Versus Digital Immigrants

In understanding the differences in the worlds that you and your daughter are facing, it important to know and understand the distinction between what Marc Prensky (2001) termed *digital natives* and *digital immigrants*. Digital immigrants describe anyone born before 1983, who came into the world of technology at a later age. Their "accents" are heavier than digital natives'. For example, they may ask a colleague whether she received an e-mail or text and use full words and sentences rather than abbreviations when texting. Digital natives are those born after 1983. From an early age, they were playing on the Internet, laptops, iPhones, iPads, and PlayStations. They are experts at text messaging, blogging, and using social media. They are fluent in the language of technology, as they communicate in real time with peers and adapt quickly to the changes introduced in the world of technology.

How Are Teens Communicating?

Texting is the primary mode of communication among teens. This is followed closely by social networking, e-mailing, and using apps. Teens prefer to text message rather than make phone calls, because it is faster, easier, and more fun. The average number of texts exchanged each month among females is 4,050 (Nielsen Mobile Report 2010). Closely behind texting is social networking. Here are just a few of the social media sites that teen girls may frequent:

Texting Apps

- **Kik:** Allows free texting. There are no limits on how many texts one can send, and the texts do not show up on the child's phone history. One concern is that there is a blog community where users submit photos or full names, dangerously revealing personal information.
- **ooVoo:** Free video and voice-message application. Users can chat in large groups.
- **WhatsApp:** App for sending free text messages, audio messages, and videos. These may all be sent to large groups.
- **GroupMe:** Texting app that does not charge fees. Users can send photos and videos.

Microblogging Apps and Sites

- **Facebook:** An online social-networking service. It attracts an older crowd and is infrequently used by teens.

- **Instagram:** More popular with adolescents, particularly females. Users snap, edit, and share photos and have the option of sending brief videos to their followers. Users can apply filters and make their photos more artistic. Teens are very focused on getting "likes." The number of likes one gets may dictate your daughter's mood and encourage competitiveness among her peers. Also, photos and videos are public unless your daughter specifies otherwise in her privacy settings.
- **Twitter:** Microblogging site that allows brief (140-character) messages called tweets. Teens can make public tweets, and posts can spread very rapidly.
- **Vine:** Users post short video clips. Videos are often inappropriate and show graphic images of people who are nude or using drugs. If the user does not adjust her settings, the videos are automatically made public. The receiver does not have to have an account to get a message.
- **Tumblr:** Users can post virtual scrapbook photos, texts, audio clips, and videos. They can create short blogs called tumblr blogs which, if made public, can be seen by anyone. Pornography is easy to access, and posts can be reblogged. This means that whatever your daughter writes can be reposted to the public.
- **Ask.fm:** A popular social-networking site where users can ask questions and remain anonymous. Often cyberbullying can result, since derogatory comments are frequently posted.
- **YouNow:** Teens can watch live videos and comment, with the goal of gaining online popularity. However, because it's live, teens can respond to viewers in real time and may broadcast themselves at inappropriate times.
- **Pheed:** Teens use this to connect and express themselves.

Secretive Apps

- **Snapchat:** Places a time limit on photos or texts to be viewed before they disappear. Teens can use this to send embarrassing or racy pictures of themselves, assuming that the posts are temporary. However, the pictures are still saved on a server somewhere, and the pictures can still be transmitted. The same issue applies to sexting, which is sending messages to someone that are highly explicit and insinuate the desire to have sex with them.

- **Burn Note:** Messaging app that "erases" messages within a short time frame. It is limited to text messages only. The concern is that the app can facilitate covert, harmful communications.
- **Yik Yak:** App in which users post brief comments to the geographically closest five hundred posters. Posters are often within a one- or two-mile radius of each other's location. Concerns are that the posts can be a vehicle for cyberbullying and can reveal a user's location.
- **Whisper:** App that encourages users to confess what is on their minds and to reveal their desires and experiences. Due to assumed anonymity, users feel freer to share their information. Concerns are that the content will be sexual in nature and that the assumption of anonymity will not be met.
- **Poof:** An app that allows users to make all the other apps on their phone disappear. Although this app no longer exists, there are similar apps that are often created so that teens can hide their apps from their parents.

Chatting, Meeting, and Dating Apps

- **Omegle:** App and chat site that pairs two people in either a text or video chat. Topics can range from music and sports to sex. The age limit is loosely enforced, and your teen may be paired in a live chat room with someone looking for sex.
- **MeetMe:** Not intended to be a dating app, but users are paired with and can "admire" others. Concerns are that personal details are required to participate, such as a zip code and location.
- **Skout:** A flirting app for teens and adults. Users are placed in age-appropriate groups. This may be a suitable site for a teen to meet someone, since the posts are grouped and moderated; however, there is no way for anyone to verify a user's age.
- **Tinder:** A messaging app where one can also post photos. This is used to browse for dates in a nearby location. Concerns are that it is location based, encouraging hookups with a nearby stranger. Matches are made when both parties swipe—or indicate approval of—each other's profile photo.
- **Blendr:** Another flirting app used to meet new people through GPS location services. Messages, photos, and videos are sent, and the "hotness" of

the users is rated. A major issue of concern is that there are no authentication requirements; thus, sexual predators have access to minors.

Site for Parents to Monitor Texts

- **TeenSafe:** An app that lets parents view their teen's social-network activity and any text messages they have sent or received, even if the posts have apparently been deleted.

Impact of Technology Use

In traversing the landscape that teens use to communicate, it is essential to understand the forms of technology they use and how the technology impacts their relationships, self-esteem, and the manner in which they communicate. This presents challenges to parents, since they are expected to help teens balance the issues presented by social media with real-time pressures. Some of these challenges include cyberbullying, sexting, obsessively taking selfies, and difficulty handling stress and down time. Parents have to learn how to balance the act of monitoring their daughter's behavior without hovering over her like a helicopter.

Impact of Technology on Teen Relationships

Pilar and her parents related to me the experience she had when she posted a status update on social media. Pilar, a seventeen-year-old senior in high school, had recently broken up with the girl she was dating and was also feeling a great deal of stress about getting into college. She posted a song about "wanting all the pain to end." Pilar was shy and had difficulty reaching out to friends for support. She posted the song in an effort to connect with others and to share with them the pain she was experiencing as a result of the loss. A few concerned classmates saw the post and showed it to their parents. The adults followed up by forwarding the posts to school officials.

Pilar was not aware of all of this until the principal called her parents, and the school psychologist (whom she had never met) conducted a suicide assessment. Pilar reported to me that she was mortified by the whole situation, since she had no intention of hurting herself but now felt as if she did something wrong by expressing herself. The questioning from the school and her family made her feel compelled to tell the school psychologist what was happening. However, in explaining this, she disclosed that she was in a relationship with another teen girl, something she was not ready to disclose to anyone.

Pilar's intention was to connect with others about the feelings of loss over the breakup with her girlfriend, but she was not yet prepared to disclose that she was in a same-sex relationship. Her social-media posts were misinterpreted. Because her community was concerned about her posts, Pilar was required to reveal personal information before she was prepared to do so.

In this situation, Pilar's community was responding the best it could to ensure her safety. As was shown in this situation, the areas most affected by technology use are communication and relationships. Whereas teens formerly communicated face to face to navigate relationships, teens of today are doing so through a screen—specifically, a phone. Therefore, they do not have access to social cues such as facial expressions and changes in voice intonation. Also, messages via text are easily misinterpreted, and teens are often unaware of the risks they are taking when they communicate in this manner.

Teens' overuse of technology often results in overstimulation of the auditory and visual senses and understimulation of other essential senses. For example, overexposure may lead to less bodily integration and motor development, decreased ability to self-soothe and self-regulate, decreased attention span, and less use of the imagination. Additionally, technology is impacting the way girls feel about themselves and how they relate to others.

Impact of Social Media on Self-Esteem

Josie, age sixteen, had been in recovery from bulimia for one year. She sat in my office with a distraught look on her face. She stated, "Listen, I know you don't like me to use my phone in your office, but I'm just waiting for this response to my post." After much pleading on her part, I explained the importance of being present in the session and assured Josie that she could check her phone after she left the session. Josie seemed angry. When I pressed her further, she recounted the events that recently occurred.

She told me that she had a crush on someone at another school and that she was waiting to see who his "WCW" was going to be. She was speaking so fast, with so many acronyms, I had to slow her down.

"Josie," I asked, feeling somewhat antiquated, "I'm sorry, but can you tell me what WCW is?" She stared at me, laughed, and said, "Uh, Woman Crush Wednesday." She then explained that she had been following this guy's posts every Wednesday, but that all his WCWs were tall women with brown hair (Josie had red hair) and that they were "much skinnier than me." All the women he was hashtagging on his WCWs were models or actresses. Additionally, she saw a picture posted of this guy at a party with some of her friends, none of whom had informed her of the event. This caused Josie to feel angry at her friends for not including her, especially since they knew about her feelings for this young man. Josie continued to tell me that she was doing well in her recovery but that she was considering dyeing her hair brown and going back on a diet, just to "lose a few pounds."

Although networking allows your daughter to stay in touch with her friends, there can also be unintended consequences that parents need to be aware of. One issue that can trouble teens is the popularity that results from posts—and the converse, as well. After posting a picture, your daughter may stay glued to her phone just to see how many comments or likes she gets, and if she is dissatisfied with the number, she can feel terrible about herself. This is so rampant that sites are now selling "likes" so that teens can shore up their popularity. Additionally, comments made by peers about your daughter's pictures or posts can be highly insensitive and can adversely affect her reputation, not just with other peers, but also with colleges and potential employers. In other words, teens need to be aware of the consequences of the material they put online.

Impact of Social Media on Self-Esteem

Cyberbullying, which will be discussed in the next chapter, has become more of a problem with the development of technology. Teens make comments online that they would never utter in person. Posting photos of oneself may result in degrading responses that further diminish the self-esteem of the teen who posted her photo. Teens may post comments about others without considering the consequences. Some seemingly innocent comments made about a photo can snowball into intense arguments between teens and reach the point of bullying. Additionally, your daughter can feel left out or saddened if she is not invited to a party that is posted online.

Impact of Technology Use on Teen Communication

You may notice that your daughter spends a great deal of time in her bedroom. Much of this time may be devoted to phone use, since she is likely sending texts or sharing and commenting on photos. Prior to the digital age, teens spent their down time communicating with one another as well; however, it was more common that they were speaking on a standard phone or were gathering in public spaces, such as malls. Although hanging out in malls may have seemed like an aimless activity at the time, teens were, in fact, gaining valuable communication skills in real time and were able to read each other's social cues, body language, and voice intonations. Communicating with phones reduces these opportunities and often produces less socially skilled teens. Additionally, messages sent via text or post are often misinterpreted and produce their own set of concerns.

Communicating through phones avoids some risks associated with in-person communication. Maybe your daughter feels more comfortable confronting a friend with whom she has a conflict and whose anger she does not wish to experience face to face. Also, asking someone out on a date in person can be a very intimidating but significant experience. With social media, face-to-face interactions are largely avoided. Thus digital communication may not adequately prepare teens for the intense emotions that come with real-time personal relationships or even for the social interactions they will face when they enter the workforce.

Tips to Help your Daughter Manage Tech Time

In order to help your daughter be more in tune with her tech time and how she uses it, consider the following suggestions:

- **Be a model for your daughter:** If your daughter sees that you are constantly on your phone, she will feel entitled to do the same. Be as present with her as possible, limiting your own time on your phone. This should encourage her to develop a more balanced pattern of technology use.
- **Implement tech-free time:** Establish family times that are device free. Try to make dinner into a tech-free evening experience. Set boundaries on when your daughter can use her devices, particularly limiting their use at bedtime.
- **Talk to your daughter:** Engage her in face-to-face conversations as much as possible. Texting throughout the day to stay in touch makes sense, but once you are together, engage her in as much actual conversation as possible. It is still the best kind of communication.
- **Discuss online etiquette:** Talk to your daughter about how harmful gossipy or demeaning posts can be to other people. Be sure your daughter also understands that anything posted online can produce a permanent electronic trail and can have adverse long-term consequences for her or for others.
- **Devise ground rules on technology use:** Work together with your daughter to devise the rules she needs to abide by in her online life. This agreement should include the maximum amount of time she is allowed to spend online daily and the requirement that she post in a respectful manner.
- **Be aware of your daughter's online practices:** Be in tune with the sites your daughter frequents, and know who her online friends are. Be certain that her friends are people she actually knows and are not virtual strangers. Come to an agreement that you will regularly check to see who her online friends are out of a concern for her safety.
- **Be aware of your own online behaviors:** Just as you can check on your daughter's online activities, she is able to check on yours, if the posts are public. Be a positive role model for your daughter, and be aware of what you are posting online as a model for her behavior.
- **Set limits on phone use:** If your daughter's phone use is interfering with other activities, set limits on when she may use it. You can require that she only use her device after her homework is complete, not while she is supposed to be sleeping, and, most importantly, not while she is operating a motor vehicle.

- **Educate your daughter about the permanence of her online reputation:** Many teens do not realize that once they post something online, it may be permanent. They may not be aware that their posts can be seen by future colleges or employers, and that once something is on the web, it often cannot be removed. Explain to her the ramifications of her online presence.
- **Teach your daughter about stranger danger:** Explain to your daughter that the people she meets online are, in reality, strangers and that communicating with them is often unsafe.

What are some ways that you limit your own tech use?

_____

_____

_____

_____

_____

_____

_____

What are some ways that you can set limits for your daughter?

_____

_____

_____

CHAPTER 12

Relational Aggression, Bullying, and Fitting in with the Crowd

One of the most significant components of your daughter's world is where she stands socially. Her social status can cause her a great deal of stress and anxiety. Your daughter's current mood may be dictated by what is happening in her friendship circles. When things are going well with her friends, she may feel on top of the world. When she is not in good standing with her peers, her mood may decline significantly. This may be the case despite whatever else is occurring in her life. Some parents have lamented, in their conversations with me, that while vacationing with their teenage daughters in beautiful, scenic places, all their daughters could focus on was what was going at home, fearful that they were missing out on some great party or other social event.

Take a moment to reflect on how well you fit in with your peers when you were your daughter's age. Summarize your experiences:

_____

_____

_____

_____

Societal Expectations

Physical aggression is expected from boys and is often commended in our society. Boys frequently hear phrases such as "don't be a wuss" or "always hit back." Male aggression is sometimes regarded as a legitimate means of expressing anger. Girls, by comparison, are expected to behave politely and to be "nice" in almost all situations. Girls usually do not exhibit anger outwardly. Instead, they socialize by expressing feelings and forming deep emotional bonds with each other. Bullying, when it occurs, is often subtle and centered on social status. The social structure is analogous to that of a queen bee with a group of followers. The leader holds most of the power and is able to control the other girls' behavior. She determines who will be her followers and who will be her victims. She often has a group of loyalists. Followers are often fearful of upsetting the leader and becoming victims themselves.

The reasons teenage girls bully each other vary. One reason may be social insecurity. If a teenage girl is uncertain of her social status, she may bully another girl in order to avoid becoming a victim herself. This may also increase her social status with the "in" group. Additionally, a teenage girl might observe bullying behavior at home and imitate it as a means of gaining control over other people. If she is experiencing any type of abuse or neglect at home, she is more likely to direct her anger toward others. Some people have personality traits—such as lack of empathy and a need to dominate—that make them more inclined to bully and taunt others.

In both male and female social makeups, there is desire for status and control, but each gender meets its goals in different ways. With boys, the process is more overt; with girls, it is more clandestine. Girls may not be physically aggressive toward each other, but they can harm each other through more subtle acts such as forming cliques, shunning each other, and spreading false rumors. These behaviors are less obvious to teachers and parents and may fly under the radar of bullying-prevention programs. If the girls were physically aggressive toward each other, the issue would be addressed on the spot, and punitive consequences could be put into place. The covert nature of these behaviors often allows them to continue unnoticed.

In addition to the acts described above, common examples of bullying behavior among girls include the following:

- Verbal harassment
- Overt and covert threats
- The use of social media and pranks to humiliate victims
- Duplicity in friendships

Commonly, girls who are bullied experience difficulties in school. They often achieve low grades and are frequently absent from school, even if they are not ill on the days they miss. They are often absent from after school events and sit by themselves at lunch and on the school bus. They may have health issues, such as headaches, and psychological problems, such as depression, low self-esteem, and suicidal thoughts. In extreme cases, they may engage in self-injury.

Relational Aggression Defined

Teenage girls place a great deal of value on social connectedness. This starts as early as the preschool years and tends to peak during adolescence. When harm is inflicted on peer relationships, through exclusion, physical or covert aggression, or online or in-person gossip, the effects can be distressing. The term for this process and its outcomes is *relational aggression*, and it can cause self-esteem to decline significantly.

Relational Aggression Can be Subtle and Have Grave Consequences

Angela, age thirteen, was referred to me by her school counselor. The school reported that Angela, formerly a top student with a great number of friends, had been truant from school. Her grades had declined significantly, and although she was typically a happy, spirited teen, she seemed much more withdrawn, lately. Her teachers and parents had grown increasingly worried about her, and although the school was originally concerned about family issues, an assessment revealed nothing unusual at home that could have led to Angela's deterioration.

It took several months for Angela to open up to me about what was going on in her life. Then, slowly, her story began to unwind. Since second grade, Angela had been friends with Carrie. Carrie just had an air about her that made people want to hang out with her. She always had the best toys when they were younger. Whenever Angela slept over at Carrie's house, they got to stay up really late, eating all kinds of junk food. Carrie's parents never stopped the kids from watching scary movies or even R-rated ones. Carrie always had the coolest clothes, and she could get anyone to do anything for her. With Carrie, Angela felt safe and protected. Angela was willing to do what it took to maintain her friendship with Carrie, even if it meant stealing, on occasion, or hurting someone's feelings. It was just worth it.

Since second grade, Carrie and Angela shared all their secrets. Carrie even told Angela that she wet her bed occasionally, which was why she had a plastic sheet underneath her bed sheet. Angela swore she would never tell anyone. They even did the blood-sister exchange—they were friends for life. Nevertheless, things began to change during the current school year. Carrie started getting even more popular and paid less attention to Angela. Angela told me that she tried even harder to get Carrie's attention, but that the more she tried, the less Carrie responded to her. One time, Angela tried to get Carrie to laugh at the lunch table by bringing up an incident in which they stole together. Carrie froze and called Angela a liar in front of all the other girls at the table. The next day, at lunch, Carrie and the girls she normally sat with were at another table. When Angela tried to sit with them, they made no room for her. Carrie started teasing Angela, telling her that she had "really nasty pimples."

One day when Angela got to school, there was a bottle of Clearasil acne cream in her locker, and the words "zit face" were painted on her locker. Angela never told anyone. Another time, there was a text message from a cute boy in the ninth grade asking Angela to the school dance. When she replied "yes," she found the words "Just kidding, zit face" posted on her Instagram. Angela was distraught and immediately deleted her Instagram account in order to avoid further embarrassment. This was the point at which we began our work.

Bullying among Teenage Girls Can Be Difficult to Detect

Since there were no physical bruises or evidence of the harassment Angela experienced, Angela's situation was difficult for school officials to identify. Often such cases are written off as typical growing pains that kids need to work out for themselves. Adults are often slow to react, if they act at all, to nonphysical bullying incidents among girls.

The following could be signs that your daughter is a victim of relational aggression:

- Change in her appetite or eating habits
- Decreased interest in school and schoolwork
- Decline in grades
- Unexplained absences from school, perhaps even without your knowledge
- Difficulty falling or staying asleep
- Stomachaches, headaches, or other somatic complaints
- Increased requests or excuses to stay home from school
- Sudden withdrawal from family and social activities
- Major changes in her wardrobe
- Change in the group of girls she typically spends time with
- A sudden need for extra money for "school lunches"
- Increased anxiety
- Change from being happy and secure to being moody and depressed
- Increased isolation

It is also possible that your daughter may be the perpetrator of relational aggression. It is not uncommon for teens to switch roles. If they were bullied at one time, they may later become the bully.

Here are some signs that your daughter could be the aggressor.

- She seems to have extra money or new belongings without an explanation.
- She is quick to blame others.
- She will not accept responsibility for her actions.
- She has friends who bully other girls.
- She needs to win or be the best at everything.

Pack Behavior and Girls in the Middle

Since bullying behavior often occurs in groups, there are those who lead and those who follow. Often there are nice kids who, unfortunately, comply with the bullying behaviors of the leader. They may disagree with the behavior of the leader but lack the skills to resist or are afraid to stand up to the leader. This, in turn, makes the victim feel as though most people are against her and strengthens the power of the bully. If adults do not intervene, the followers and victim may feel even more incapable of responding properly.

Tips to Help Your Daughter Handle Bullying If She Is a Bystander

- Encourage your daughter to intervene by confronting the bully and telling her to cease the unkind behaviors.
- Let your daughter know that by ignoring the bullying, or being a bystander, she is complicit in the bullying process.
- If your daughter does not feel comfortable intervening, tell her to inform an adult about the situation.

How to Prevent and Respond to Relational Aggression

Before intervention can begin, it is important to identify the basis of the problem. Is the bullying occurring because the needs of the tormenter are not being met or because the bully has an overwhelming need to belong to a group? Try to understand and respond to those possibilities before intervening. This can be done through the counseling process, which identifies the underlying reasons for bullying behaviors, and teaches more humane ways of meeting the bullying person's needs.

Tips to Prevent Bullying or to Respond to It Appropriately

- **Be involved with your school:** Many schools have antibullying programs. Be sure that all relevant people are trained to appropriately carry out the intervention, as stated. Ensure that the curriculum covers relational-aggression issues among girls and that the school faculty know how to recognize and respond to the signs of bullying.
- **Teach all children healthy communication skills:** Teens need the skills to deal with and express their conflicts. Messages are often misinterpreted, particularly with electronic communications.
- **Provide good examples of social interactions:** Bullyish and cliquish behaviors can, and do, occur between adults. Be in tune with how you

treat other people, especially people with less status than you have. Note also how you treat the family pet. Your kids are watching you!

- **Role-play:** Act out various scenarios with your daughter. Teach her how to recognize and respond to a variety of social situations in a manner that will avoid relational aggression.
- **Teach anger-management skills:** Most teens, particularly girls, do not have the tools necessary to cope with anger. Teach your daughter it is okay to feel angry, but then provide her with the skills to express anger appropriately.
- **Educate yourself:** Stay current on social-media issues and bullying-prevention programs. Learn to recognize the signs of bullying, whether your child is the aggressor, victim, or bystander.
- **Keep a close eye on your daughter's behavior at home:** Set limits, calmly, on acts of aggression or exclusion you see against friends, siblings, or other children in your home. If you notice any type of relationship aggression, talk to your daughter about other ways she can deal with these situations appropriately.

If you find that your daughter is, in fact, being bullied, here are tools to help her to deal with this problem:

- **Maintain other relationships:** Encourage your daughter to maintain connections with friends outside of school to foster a larger support system.
- **Allow a safe space for her to talk to you:** Avoid emotional outbursts. Just being a calm presence, without a plan to march immediately into the school and ream out the parents of the other girls, will encourage your daughter to open up to you more.
- **Seek outside support:** Request the help of a therapist to provide opportunities for your daughter to have others to talk to and to learn the skills for coping.
- **Inform the school:** Let your daughter's principal, school counselor, and teachers know the situation. Let them partner with you in coming up with a plan for keeping your daughter safe.
- **Build your daughter's confidence:** Continue to provide a safe and nurturing home where your daughter has the opportunity to express her needs and build her strengths. The more her confidence develops, the more likely she will be able to develop healthy friendships with peers.

- **Continue to communicate with the school:** Never stop communicating with the school, and make sure the officials know that this problem is a priority for you. Work with the staff as a team, and ask them what they have observed and can suggest. Inform the school personnel about changes you have observed in your daughter's situation.

Cyberbullying

Cyberbullying is another form of relational aggression. It entails harming another person through the use of technology or social media. This method of relational aggression is particularly toxic because bullies can easily spread rumors and can create online cliques and gossip about their targets, anonymously.

Because teens are now so engaged with their phones, they are particularly aware of what is taking place socially at all times of the day. They will reach the depths of the emotional roller coaster when they see photos of groups in which they were not included or when they notice that someone has unfriended them without explanation.

Cyberbullying compounds the complicated dynamics of jealousy and rejection that teens face each day, since people have access to their phones twenty-four seven. Prior to this era, youngsters had a reprieve from these interactions for a substantial part of the day. The following are ways in which cyberbullying can be carried out:

- Pretending to be someone else online to get the victim in trouble or to embarrass her
- Creating a website for the purpose of teasing someone
- Sending insulting texts or e-mails
- Enticing someone into sharing embarrassing information online
- Starting rumors about someone online
- Posting derogatory comments about others on social-media sites
- Making threats through the use of technology
- Posting personal or embarrassing photos or videos of someone else

Teens are likely to use cyberbullying because they can usually avoid punitive consequences for their behavior. Often it is easier to write a quick post than to say something hurtful in someone's physical presence. The consequences of cyberbullying for the victim, however, are very harmful and may result in humiliation and isolation.

Consequences of Cyberbullying

Kendra came to my office the summer before her junior year began. Her parents had moved her to a private school due to several unpleasant incidents that occurred in the public school the previous year. During her sophomore year, Kendra started dating a senior. Her friends at the time became increasingly distant and even destructive. One of the girls watched her log into her phone and memorized her password. The girl then sent messages to Kendra's boyfriend, telling him that she wanted to break up with him. Another friend took pictures of Kendra changing in the locker room and posted them on Instagram with the hashtag #fatslut.

Kendra was devastated. When she finally told her parents, they tried to engage the school, but the school officials refused to get involved because the postings did not take place during school hours. Depressed, Kendra lost thirty pounds and vowed to start afresh at the new school she would be attending in the fall.

Tips to Prevent Cyberbullying

Here are some tips that can help protect your daughter from being cyberbullied. Instruct her to adhere to the following rules:

- She should not give out passwords or personal information, even to friends.
- She should use the privacy options on all social-networking sites so she can control who sees what she posts.
- She should not friend people online if she doesn't know them, even if they have friends in common.
- She should log out of all accounts before leaving computers, especially shared ones.

How to Help Your Daughter If She Is Being Cyberbullied:

Inform her

- not to respond to posts or e-mails if she is being bullied online—the best thing to do is to ignore the posts or block the person;
- to document all evidence of online bullying behavior;
- to involve school authorities, if appropriate;
- to report incidents of bullying to the Internet provider or phone company;
- to report the incidents to the police, if threats to use violence or post pornography are made.

CHAPTER 13

Self-Injury and Suicide

lthough they are grouped together, self-injury and suicide are very different. Most people who self-injure do not intend to kill themselves.

Self-Injury

Self-injury includes behaviors such as cutting, burning, pulling bodily hairs, punching bodily parts, and swallowing toxic substances or harmful objects. Someone may cut herself on her wrists, arms, legs, breasts, or stomach. Some people self-injure by burning their skin with a match or a cigarette. Similar to substance abuse and eating disorders, there is no single reason why adolescents self-injure. It is the case, however, that teenage girls are more likely to self-injure than are teenage boys.

Self-injury has become more widespread since the late 1990s. Rates of self-injury are difficult to measure, since the behaviors typically occur privately. One study published in the *Journal of Pediatrics*, involving 665 youths, found that 7.6 percent of third graders and 12.7 percent of ninth graders had self-injured seriously at least once (Esposito 2012). Celebrities have come out in the open about their struggles with self-injury, and there are even live video demonstrations online that glorify self-injury.

Self Injury to Feel Calm

Sofia was feeling overwhelmed. Her parents were occupied with work, and her older brother was getting ready to go to college. Sofia's friends were angry with her because they felt she did not spend as much time with them since she started dating Tye. Tye was also putting pressure on Sofia to spend more time with him and was jealously monitoring her activities. Her schoolwork was becoming unbearable.

After she saw that her friends had recently posted about her in a denigrating manner, she had had enough. Sofia grabbed a razor blade from the bathroom and ran it over her thighs. When she started to bleed, she felt relief. This is when the cycle began for her. For the next year, whenever Sofia felt overwhelmed, she repeated this same sequence. She cut in places that she thought no one would notice. Then, one day, during her yearly physical, the family doctor saw her scars, and she was referred for therapy.

When I met with Sofia, she told me that she cut herself because it "helps me to chill." She told me that the feeling of the razor or a piece of glass piercing her skin did not hurt. If anything, "it helped to make me feel okay." It also allowed her to concentrate on homework and to deal with any conflicts going on at school or with friends. Sofia was not suicidal. However, she was using self-injury as a means to cope with uncomfortable emotions.

Teens who self-injure are not necessarily suicidal. In fact, they often are not. Nevertheless, self-injury should be treated very seriously. If teens are not taught appropriate alternative coping tools, the self-injurious behaviors can become a frequent occurrence. Additionally, someone who cuts herself is at risk of losing dangerous amounts of blood, acquiring an infection, striking an artery, or in the worst of cases, dying from an incident that has gone wrong. Once the wounds heal, there are sometimes visible scars on the teen's body that she may attempt to hide from others.

Functions of Self-Injury

It may be hard to understand why someone would want to hurt herself. Self-injury actually functions in many ways for those who engage in the behavior.

Self-Soothing

Teens who self-injure often do so in order to anesthetize themselves from painful feelings. Someone who is experiencing high levels of stress and who has not, as yet, developed appropriate coping skills may find that behaviors such as cutting and scratching temporarily calm her down.

Control

If a teen feels that she lacks control in crucial areas of her life, she may regard self-injury as a means of acquiring a measure of this missing control. Paradoxically, harming herself may help her to ease the chaos and unpredictability she is experiencing.

Distraction

When a teenage girl is experiencing high levels of emotional turmoil, self-injury may distract her from painful feelings. Instead of focusing on the emotional pain, she can focus on the physical pain, which may be less overwhelming to her.

Expression

People who have problems verbally expressing feelings such as anger and sadness may self-injure as a means of communication. This may be the only way they have to express their anguish to others.

Self-Punishment

Unfortunately, some girls self-injure in order punish themselves, feeling that they deserve their self-inflicted pain. Many of the teens have a history of abuse and blame themselves instead of the perpetrators.

Other Mental-Health Concerns

Those who self-injure may have other mental-health problems that trigger such behaviors. These could include depression, bipolar disorder, eating disorders, borderline personality disorder, substance addictions, or compulsive behaviors.

Pressure

Sometimes, self-injurious behavior takes place in groups. Some teens self-injure in order to fit in with friends who are encouraging them to harm themselves.

Impact of Self-Injury

Self-injury may start as an occasional event, but with enough repetition may become a compulsion. If the person continues to engage in self-injurious behavior, the practice can become difficult to stop, comparable to ending an addiction such as smoking or abusing alcohol.

Warning Signs

The following are warning signs that your daughter might be engaged in self-injurious behaviors:

- Having multiple unexplained cuts or burns on her wrists, arms, legs, or other parts of her body
- Wearing loose clothing
- Spending long periods of time in the bathroom
- Dressing in long sleeves when the weather is warm
- Placing sharp objects (e.g., razors, scissors, objects with sharp edges) in various parts of the house
- Isolating from friends and family

What to Do If Your Daughter Is Self-Injuring

It is extremely upsetting for parents to discover that their daughter has been self-injuring. Placing the blame on the teen is not helpful. The most useful way to handle this behavior is to avoid being in denial and to acknowledge that there is a serious issue for which your daughter needs help. You should try to remain calm while securing all dangerous objects in the home.

Parents sometimes assume that when their daughter cuts herself she is suicidal and immediately take her to the emergency room. It is important to always ask first what the intention of the self-harm is and whether she is attempting to kill herself, since her safety comes first. If you believe she is attempting to kill herself, immediately take her to the nearest emergency room. If she has a deep cut that requires medical attention, she should also be taken to the hospital. Unfortunately, the attending medical staff may not have sufficient experience or expertise to deal with these issues, and the treatment is not always appropriate. In some instances, inexperienced medical staff make the assumption that the teen is cutting herself for attention. This may or may not be true.

It is important to immediately seek treatment from a professional who has experience in and is comfortable with treating self-injury in teenage girls. It might be useful for your daughter to have an individual or family therapist and to join a skills-training group in dialectical behavioral therapy. This modality helps individuals learn how to tolerate uncomfortable emotions and to deal with conflict in a healthy manner.

If issues at home are contributing to the self-injury, family therapy may also be necessary. Such therapy can give the family the tools necessary to intervene when a teen signals that she is likely to self-injure. The counseling will also teach the parents how to react properly when their daughter does self-injure. In some instances, medication might be necessary, particularly if there is a co-occurring mental-health disorder. Additionally, therapeutic interventions such as art, music, and movement therapy can be excellent modalities for self-expression, since they can help your daughter explore thoughts and feelings that she finds difficult to express in words.

Additional Ways to Support Your Daughter

- **Be a positive model for stress management:** Try to show your daughter, by example, how you manage stress in healthy ways.
- **Make time for family activities:** It is important for your daughter to feel that family time is valued and that you are working together as a unit. Make sure she is an important part of family conversations.
- **Provide opportunities for using coping tools:** If you notice your daughter is overwhelmed or is having urges to self-injure, try distractions such as taking a walk with her. Engage in the coping tools together.
- **Stay calm when your daughter shares urges with you:** If your daughter shares with you her urges to self-injure, it means that she trusts you and wants your help. Although you might be frightened when this occurs, try to stay calm. Just being composed and being able to listen can help your daughter regulate her emotions and delay or even avoid an incident of self-injury.
- **Limit technology use:** Although it was mentioned in other chapters, it is important to reemphasize this. Teens may struggle with self-injury as

a result of spending many hours on social media, viewing posts that are triggering, portraying, and glorifying self-injury. As previously mentioned, keep a close eye on your daughter's online activities.

- **Don't expect a quick fix:** Even if your daughter has sought recovery, there are still likely to be lapses. Do not view these as major setbacks, or even relapses, but as part of the process. Learn from what happened, and then help her get back on track.

Teen Suicide

With suicide the third-leading cause of death among youths aged ten to fourteen and the second-leading cause among persons aged fifteen to thirty-four, parents of teens need to take heed. Although males end their lives at nearly four times the rate that females do, females are more likely than males to have suicidal thoughts (Centers for Disease Control 2015).

Which Teenage Girls Are at Risk for Suicide?

As you know from having a young daughter and reading about the issues raised in the earlier chapters, being a teenage girl is not always easy. There are wonderful times to be had, but there are also times of considerable stress and confusion, as girls are in a limbo stage between being a girl and being a woman.

Teen Vulnerability

Teenage girls who also have mental-health or drug-abuse issues are more likely to have suicidal thoughts. They may have a difficult time dealing with stressors in life and contemplate suicide as a way to escape these issues.

Risk Factors for Teen Suicide

Factors that increase the risk of teen suicide include the following:

- A family history of mental-health problems or suicide attempts
- A psychiatric disorder, such as depression, anxiety, or bipolarity
- A previous suicide attempt

- A history of violence or sexual abuse
- Identifying as an LGBTQ individual in a family or community that is not supportive
- Ability to access means of suicide through firearms or medications or other means
- Drug or alcohol abuse
- Isolation
- Loss of a close family member
- Frequent conflict with close friends or family members
- Unwanted pregnancy
- Witnessing a suicide
- A history of incarceration

I began seeing Michelle as a result of several suicidal threats she had revealed to her parents. Michelle was adopted, and her parents were divorced and living in two different states. Several months prior to seeing me, Michelle left her mother's home in New Jersey to live with her father and stepmother in Pennsylvania. The move was made to give Michelle a fresh start at a new school, after Michelle had experienced several conflicts at her former school.

Although Michelle's parents communicated regularly, they had markedly different sets of rules at each house. Michelle's father permitted her to indulge in material items and gave her an unlimited allowance. With her mother, she was required to work and contribute to the family income. Michelle's father and stepmother often had heated and extended arguments about how the father indulged Michelle. The parents also argued when Michelle came home after 2:00 a.m. and when she smoked marijuana in the house. During one of the parents' arguments, Michelle screamed, "You'll all be happier when I am gone." Michelle's father and stepmother were at a loss as to how to handle these statements and simply brushed them aside. More recently, however, Michelle, swallowed several medications at once, which prompted a trip to the emergency room. Michelle survived, but the incident left Michelle's parents feeling frightened and helpless. The first step in the process was to help Michelle and her family to find ways to keep her safe.

Cases similar the one described above are not uncommon. Teenage girls deal with a great number of stressors and often have difficulty regulating their emotions and communicating their needs. Most troubling, it is hard to know whether someone really wants to die or is simply making a plea for attention. Regardless, every threat to commit suicide must be taken seriously.

Warning Signs of Suicide

The subject of suicide is not an easy one to broach. There are often stigmas associated with the topic, as victims are blamed for being "selfish," or their families are blamed for creating an environment in which their daughters want to end their lives. Most often, teens who kill themselves have already given warning signs, such as the following:

- Having a preoccupation with death
- Having a history of drug or alcohol use
- Giving away personal belongings
- Dropping hints such as "I won't be around much longer"
- Exhibiting abrupt changes in mood
- Engaging in reckless or impulsive behavior
- Showing signs of self-injury (for example, cuts, burns, or bruises)

How to Prevent Suicide

Talking openly can have a beneficial impact in helping a teen who is considering suicide. Teens who have made suicide attempts have usually given some warning signs. It is important, then, to know what to look for, so your daughter can get assistance. Do not be passive about asking her what she needs. Be proactive in letting her know that you are there to help her and that you will take whatever steps are necessary to get her relief.

It is also important to pay attention to your daughter and notice any signs she may be sending out. If your daughter opens up to you, take her feelings seriously. Although an altercation with a friend might not seem like a major problem to you, to her it can be all-consuming, particularly if she is already feeling depressed. It is important not to trivialize how she is feeling.

If she does not feel that she can open up to you, try to identify a third party such as a therapist or clergy member. Even if you believe some of the threats are just cries for attention, take them seriously and act on them as if they are genuine. If teenagers are ignored when they are in search of attention, the chances of attempting suicide increase. If your daughter has an immediate plan to end her life and the means to carry it out, she should be taken to the emergency room or a crisis treatment center. If she does not have an immediate plan, it is important to pay attention to your daughter and find out what she is feeling. Other preventative measures include:

- **Limiting access to dangerous items:** If you have firearms in the home, remove them from the home immediately. Lock all medicine and liquor cabinets. Any access to such items significantly increases the risk of attempting suicide.
- **Avoiding isolation:** Encourage your daughter to spend time with others. Being alone may increase suicidal tendencies.
- **Working with a team:** If your daughter is working with a mental-health professional, school counselor, or others, communicate with them, and seriously consider their recommendations.

What to Do If Your Daughter Is Suicidal

If you believe your daughter is experiencing suicidal thoughts, it is important to refer her to an experienced professional, immediately. A good referral source is your family-medicine practitioner. If your daughter later feels less depressed, she may want to cancel a therapy appointment that's already scheduled. Try to convince her to keep the appointment, so she can develop a relationship with a professional who will teach her the skills necessary to cope with suicidal thoughts and other stressors should they arise again. Be sure to provide the therapist with a family history of mental-health issues, as well as any other significant stressors occurring in the home.

When talking to your daughter about the topic, openly use terms such as "suicide" or "kill yourself." For example, you might say, "I have noticed you making a lot of comments about not wanting to be here. Have you been having thoughts about trying to kill yourself?" Do not dance around the topic. Research indicates that asking direct questions *will not* plant the idea of suicide in your daughter's head. Despite the fears you are experiencing, it is important to remain calm during these conversations and reassure your daughter that you are there to support her and will get her the help she needs.

When a Peer Carries Out a Suicide

If your daughter has lost a close friend or classmate to suicide, this will likely be a very disturbing event for her. Acknowledge that she may be experiencing a wide array of emotions, ranging from guilt for not doing more to help her friend, to anger for what she regards as a selfish and immature act. Whatever the case, acknowledge your daughter's feelings, and give her time to process them.

CONCLUDING COMMENTS

Being a teenage girl can be challenging at times and can be all the more so for her, sometimes, baffled parents. Hopefully by reading this book you will have a greater understanding as to why teenage girls behave as they do, and you will also have acquired some practical tips to help guide you through this journey.

Although I have described many concerning issues throughout this book, it is important *not* to become overwhelmed with everything that can go wrong as you raise your teenage daughter. Both you and your daughter are bound to make mistakes; it would be abnormal if you didn't. This is a learning process for all parties. These years are the time for identity building and growth, as well as the acquisition of healthy coping behaviors for your daughter.

Aside from the challenges faced by the modern teenage girl, it is also important to recognize that the teen years are usually an exciting stage of life for girls—full of self-exploration, adventure, and heightened awareness. Parents are faced with the challenges of setting limits and helping to keep their daughters safe, but giving them room to grow, all while maintaining a close personal connection to them. Most parents will look back fondly at their daughter's teen years, and all parties will share a laugh as they reminisce about the process of going from a sobbing, giggly teen to a young woman who is thinking about furthering her education, beginning a career, and possibly starting her own family some time in the future.

Ultimately, you can help your daughter navigate the wavy waters she will experience during the teen years. The purpose of this book is to give you some tools that will ease this process. Yes, you and your daughter will experience some bumps along the road, but you can teach her how to cope with life's stressors and you can empower her with the ability to deal effectively with these challenges. With some effort, we can help young women to understand that the goals of adolescence are to

- be flexible,
- problem solve,
- read people correctly,
- regulate feelings,
- handle disappointment, and
- enjoy successes.

Bear in mind that you are not alone in this process. It truly takes a village to raise a child. Become familiar with your daughter's friends and engage in activities with them and their families. Get to know your daughter's teachers, coaches, and instructors. You are not in this by yourself.

But most of all, it is the connection and love you have with your daughter that will ultimately help her have a strong relationship with others and with herself. With that in mind, my hope is that you will approach these years, not with fear, but with the optimism that you are helping your daughter to go through this challenging, yet empowering and wonderful stage of life. This will likely be the most fulfilling, important, and ultimately rewarding venture you will ever experience.

ABOUT THE AUTHOR

Robin Axelrod Sabag, LCSW, is a clinical social worker, and marriage and family therapist who has been helping teens and their families to improve their communication skills and to build strong family bonds for over fifteen years. She also works with individuals and couples.

Sabag has worked in a variety of settings, including residential treatment centers and outpatient settings, and has been in private practice as the provider of clinical and oversight services. A sought-after mental-health expert, she often speaks and writes on the topic of teenage girls and has been an adjunct professor at Temple University. Additionally, Sabag has been interviewed on Philadelphia Fox 29, offering advice on how to discuss hate crimes with children.

To learn more, visit her website at www.robinsabagtherapy.com

REFERENCES

Advocates for Youth. "Parent-Child Communication Promoting Sexually Healthy Youth". http://www.advocatesforyouth.org/

Banks, Carole. 2017. "You're Grounded for Life! Why Harsh Punishments for Children and Teenagers Don't Work". Empowering Parents. https://www.empoweringparents.com/article/youre-grounded-for-life-why-harsh-punishments-for-children-and-teenagers-dont-work/

Bowen, Murray. 1992. *Family Therapy in Clinical Practice*. New York: Rowman and Littlefield Publishers, Inc.

Bradley, Michael L. 2003. *Yes, Your Teen Is Crazy! Loving Your Kid Without Losing Your Mind*. Harbor Press, Inc.

Centers for Disease Control. 2015. *Suicide Facts at a Glance*. https://www.cdc.gov/violenceprevention/pdf/suicide-datasheet-a.pdf

Child Trends. 2017. "Marijuana Use". Databank Indicator. https://www.childtrends.org/indicators/marijuana-use/

Da Silva, Julia. 2015. "Children and Electronic Media: How Much Is Too Much?" American Psychological Association. http://www.apa.org/pi/about/newsletter/2015/06/electronic-media.aspx.

Dartmouth News. 2014. "New Study: Video Games and Teen's Behavior". Office of Communications. https://news.dartmouth.edu/news/2014/08/new-study-video-games-and-teens-behavior

Dreisbach, Shaun. 2014. "How Do You Feel About Your Body." *Glamour Health*. http://www.glamour.com/story/body-image-how-do-you-feel-about-your-body.

Dove Self Esteem Project. 2017. "A Girl Should Feel Free to be Herself." http://self-esteem.dove.us/

Esposito, Lisa. "Self Harm Showing up in Elementary Schools". U.S. News. http://health.usnews.com/health-news/news/articles/2012/06/11/self-harm-showing-up-in-elementary-schools-study?offset=530

Goldenberg, L., and H. Goldenberg. 1996. *Family Therapy: An Overview*. Pacific Grove, CA: Brooks/Cole.

Heubeck, Elizabeth. WebMd. 2017. "Helping Girls with Body Image". http://www.webmd.com/beauty/features/helping-girls-with-body-image#1

Holmqvist, K., A. Frisen, and E. Anderson-Fye. 2014. "Body Image and Child Well-Being". https://www.researchgate.net/profile/Eileen_Anderson-Fye/publication/262583780_Body_Image_and_Child_Well-Being/links/570db55208aed31341cf7d62.pdf.

Huesmann, L.Rowell. 2017. "The Impact of Electronic Media Violence: Scientific Theory and Research". National Institute of Public Health Public Health. Univeristy of Michigan.

Jewish Women International. 2014. "Dating Abuse Tools for Talking to Kids". http://datingabuse.worldsecuresystems.com/

Knafo, Hannah. 2016. "The Development of Body Image in School-Aged Girls: A Review of the Literature from Sociocultural, Social Learning Theory, Psychoanalytic, and Attachment Perspectives." *The New School Psychology Bulletin*. Vol. 13, No. 2.

Lenhart, Amanda, Anderson, M., and Smith, A. 2015. *Teens, Technology and Romantic Relationships*. Pew Research Center. http://www.pewinternet.org/2015/10/01/basics-of-teen-romantic-relationships/.

Love Is Respect. 2016. *Healthy Relationships*. http://www.loveisrespect.org.

Media Influences to the Development of Body Satisfaction and Self-Esteem in Young Girls: A Prospective Study." *Development Psychology*. http://www.willettsurvey.org/TMSTN/Gender/PeerAndMediaInfluencesOnYoungGirls.pdf.

Moy, G. 2015. *Media, Family, and Peer Influence on Children's Body Image.* https://rucore.libraries.rutgers.edu/rutgers-lib/48157/PDF/1/

National Association of Anorexia Nervosa and Associated Disorders, Inc. 2017. *Eating Disorder Statistics.* http://www.anad.org/get-information/about-eating-disorders/eating-disorders-statistics/

National Institute on Drug Abuse. 2016. *Drug Facts: Marijuana.* https://www.drugabuse.gov/publications/drugfacts/marijuana.

National Institute of Mental Health. 2011. *The Teen Brain: Still Under Construction.* https://www.nimh.nih.gov/health/publications/the-teen-brain-still-under-construction/index.shtml

Nielsen Mobile Report. 2010. *Mobile Youth Around the World.* http://www.nielsen.com/us/en/insights/reports/2010/mobile-youth-around-the-world.html.

Northup, T., & Liebler, C. M. 2010. "The Good, the Bad, and the Beautiful." *Journal of Children & Media.* https://rucore.libraries.rutgers.edu/rutgers-lib/48157/PDF/1/

Parenting Strategies. 2017. "Preventing Adolescent Alcohol Misuse". http://www.parentingstrategies.net/alcohol/home/

PR Newswire. 2008. "New National Report Reveals the High Price of Low Self-Esteem". http://www.prnewswire.com/news-releases/new-national-report-reveals-the-high-price-of-low-self-esteem-65355592.html.Prensky, Marc. 2001. "Digital Natives, Digital Immigrants." *On the Horizon.* MCB University Press, Vol. 9, No. 5.

Raising Children Network. 2017. "When Puberty is Late or Early". http://raising-children.net.au/articles/puberty_early_or_late.html

Rideout, Victoria, Foehr, Ulla, and Roberts, Donald. (2010) "Generation M2 Media in the Lives of 8 to 18 Year Olds". A Kaiser Family Foundation Study. https://kaiserfamilyfoundation.files.wordpress.com/2013/04/8010.pdf